A Student's Guide
to
ELEMENTS OF PROOF

By

Ronald L. Carlson
Fuller E. Callaway Professor of Law
University of Georgia

Mat #40212200

© 2004 West, a Thomson business
     610 Opperman Drive
     P.O. Box 64526
     St. Paul, MN 55164–0526
     1–800–328–9352

ISBN 0–314–15147–8

TEXT IS PRINTED ON 10% POST
CONSUMER RECYCLED PAPER

*This book is dedicated to the Honorable Myron Bright—
judge, esteemed colleague, friend.*

*

About the book Elements of Proof

———

Skill in handling the elements of proof, and deft presentation of trial facts, are critical needs of the modern litigator. This text is dedicated to providing essential testimony for at-a-glance reference in the classroom or office, or in hearings or trials.

One of the most prominent sources for trial proofs contained in this text was R. Carlson, *Successful Techniques for Civil Trials 2d*. Many proofs were adapted from this work. Others were taken from cases, or developed by the author from law school classes as well as CLE seminars he conducted on evidence and trial practice.

Names supplied by the author in trial proofs which appear in this text do not refer to actual persons. While the facts in the model case transcripts are sometimes drawn from actual cases, the names which are included are not intended to refer to specific people or actual companies. Relation to real persons is coincidental.

Every "Q. and A." is illustrative of the kind of testimony commonly received in connection with the offered fact. As a rule, each proof will serve as a general guide for law students and lawyers as to the sort of testimony he or she will pursue in any particular case. On some proofs, we join the case in progress. Often we target the essential element of proof for the designated topic, leaving full development of the remainder of the witness' testimony for the rest of the trial.

Consistently, in some of the proofs all of the mechanical steps in approaching witnesses, making a record of displaying exhibits to opposing counsel, circulation of the exhibit to the jury, and the like appear. See, for example, the *Handwriting* proof. Again, however, for purposes of compactness, the full measure of each procedural step has been omitted from some proofs. For the full panoply of procedural elements, see the *Handwriting* entry.

Objections appear in virtually every trial scene, to test the adequacy of the foundation. Sometimes objections are made in a slightly delayed fashion in the book's transcripts so the reader can see the direction of the proposed testimony, rather than cluttering the text with early objections and offers of proof. For expanded treatment of objections (as opposed to the nonobjectionable introduction of proof which is the focus of this text), see M. Bright, R. Carlson, & E. Imwinkelried, *Objections at Trial* (2002); Gibbons, *A Student's Guide to Trial Objections* (2003).

One of the virtues of this text is its uncluttered format. By eliminating tedious detail, it seeks to place immediately at hand the key elements of trial proof needed by student and practitioner alike. Its blend of foundation elements, rule references and case authorities in a distilled package provide a unique trial guide. Whether in courses like evidence or trial practice, in mock trials or in real courtrooms, this little book can be a legal life-saver. When one's opponent intones "Objection, inadequate foundation," a quick glance at the correct page in this text will save the day.

The author is indebted to people at Thomson West Publishers. Prominent among those are Heidi Hellekson and Douglas Powell for their vision in seeing the potential for this work. Staci Herr was the editorial contact during the editing process. At the University of Georgia, Mary Fielding was flawless in her preparation of the manuscript. Research assistants Vita Maria Salvemini (class of 2005), Meredith Bunn (class of 2004), Erica Parsons (class of 2004) and Martha Kelley (class of 2003) ably checked and researched citations.

This book is devoted to the challenge of locating needed elements of factual proof in a rapid, practical manner.

RONALD L. CARLSON

How to Use This Guide

———

You can quickly find the information you need by following these steps:

Step 1. Select the topic in which you are interested from the alphabetical List of Topics beginning on the following page.

Step 2. Consult the applicable "Q. & A.", together with the accompanying Elements as well as the Case Authorities and Comments.

Step 3. Refer to the Rule Reference for federal rules provisions which either govern your topic or which serve as useful background.

Foundation Steps

Each entry in the text contains the following divisions.

•**Elements,** a summary of the distinct elements of proof which must be established in connection with each item of evidence.

•**Witness Examination,** a trial transcript demonstrating how to develop the critical elements of evidentiary foundations.

•**Rule Reference,** containing the evidentiary rule which controls the introduction of proof needed to comply with legal requirements.

•**Cases and Authorities,** incorporating recent cases adjudicating evidentiary requirements.

•**Comment,** summarizing approach needed to blend the elements into a successful mosaic of trial proof.

*

List of Topics

A Student's Guide
to
ELEMENTS OF PROOF

*

Admissions

Elements

A party's own statement may be proved against the party by establishing the following elements: 1) the witness who is on the stand heard one of the parties make a statement, and the witness identifies this party as the author of the remark; 2) the declaration is relevant to the issues at trial; 3) the trial witness is called by one party (party A) and the declaration was uttered by the opposing party (party B).

Direct Examination

Q. (by plaintiff's attorney) Mr. Green, when did you arrive at the scene of the auto collision which is the subject of this case?

A. It was only a minute or so after it occurred.

Q. What did you see?

A. I got out of my car, and the drivers of the two cars which were involved in the crash were out and walking around.

Q. Did you talk to anyone?

A. Yes. I walked up to that man (indicating defendant driver for the record) and asked what happened?

Q. Let the record show that the witness indicated the defendant. Did he respond?

A. Yes. He said....

Objection by defense: Hearsay, your honor.

Response by Plaintiff's attorney: Admission by party opponent, your honor.

1

Court: Overruled.

Q. (by plaintiff's attorney) You may answer the question. What did the defendant say?

A. He was shaking his head, and stated: "I don't know why I ran that stop sign. I just didn't look, I guess."

Rule Reference

Federal Rule of Evidence 801(d)(2)(A) provides that a statement is not hearsay if the statement is offered against a party and is "the party's own statement, in either an individual or a representative capacity."

Cases and Authorities

United States v. Reed, 227 F.3d 763, 769–70 (7th Cir. 2000) underlines the point that a party's own statement may be used against him. This is the rule in both civil and criminal cases. The admissions doctrine supplies a generous avenue to admissibility. Where the doctrine applies, it overcomes a hearsay objection.

Admissions may consist of factual statements. In addition, admissions may be in the form of opinions and also may be the product of less than first-hand knowledge. There is no rule that a party's own admission must be based on personal knowledge, see *Blackburn v. United Parcel Service, Inc.,* 179 F.3d 81, 96 (3d Cir. 1999)(admissions need not be based upon personal knowledge), nor are admissions controlled by the opinion rule, see *United States v. Bakshinian,* 65 F.Supp.2d 1104, 1109 (C.D. Cal. 1999) (opinions are freely admissible when made by a party-opponent).

Written admissions, see *United States v. Pickard,* 278 F.Supp.2d 1217, 1234 (D. Kan. 2003)(holding letters written by defendant after arrest which contained admissions against interest were not hearsay and were admissible under Fed. R.

Evid. 801(d)(2)(A)); *Zeigler v. Fisher–Price, Inc.*, 302 F.Supp.2d 999 (N.D. Iowa 2004)(holding voluntary press release announcing recall of Power Wheels toy vehicles because electrical components [of Power Wheels toy vehicles] can overheat and cause fires was admissible in product liability action against Fisher–Price as admission by manufacturer under Fed. R. Evid. 801(d)(2)(A), (B), and (C)).

Comment

Admissions can be written as well as oral. Frequently party A endeavors to introduce a writing authored by party B under the admissions rule. A letter from Party B to Party A prior to the onset of the litigation and containing damaging admissions provides an example of this sort of evidence. Once introduced, the party who made the admission can explain, justify or contradict it.

Judicial admissions, on the other hand, are often deemed to be binding. Judicial admissions may arise from a party's statement in its pleadings, response to discovery requests, or from careless remarks during closing arguments. Binding judicial admissions are self-injuring statements, either oral or written, made in the course of judicial proceedings.

Pretrial declarations by accused persons are admissions which may be used against the defendant in criminal prosecutions. However, in criminal cases custodial admissions—those made by the accused after arrest and secured while the defendant is in custody—must be shown by the prosecutor to have been secured after compliance with the dictates of the *Miranda* decision. Where the defendant is confined and is interrogated, a resulting confession or admission by the defendant must be preceded by constitutional warnings. A valid waiver of Fifth and Sixth Amendment rights must be obtained. See *Confessions*, infra.

More on admissions, see *Adoptive Admissions* and *Agent Admissions*, both infra. For admissions containing references to insurance, see the entry for *Insurance Information*.

Adoptive Admissions

Elements

An admission by silence may be created against a party who remained silent in the face of an accusation. Such admissions are proved up when the opponent establishes the following elements: 1) at a prior time someone made an accusation, or directed an accusatory question, to one of the parties in the current proceeding (party B); 2) the opposing party (party A) calls the accuser to the stand, or another person who heard the accuser make the accusation, as a trial witness; 3) when the accusation was originally made, the accused party apparently heard the accusation and stood mute; 4) the accusation was made under conditions which would prompt an innocent person to react with a denial, or a protestation of innocence, if the accusation was false.

Direct Examination

Q. **(by prosecutor)** Mr. Bishop, where was the defendant when you talked to him?

A. In Rocky's Tap. It was a couple of nights before he was arrested. We were drinking together at the bar.

Q. What did you say?

A. I knew his uncle had been killed. I said to the defendant "Lefty, that guy who was killed the other night. I have an idea that you did it!"

Q. What response, if any, did the defendant make?

A. He didn't say a word. But he did give me a big smile.

Defense: Move to strike.

Response by Prosecutor: Adoptive admission, your honor.

Court: Motion denied.

Rule Reference

Federal Rule of Evidence 801(d)(2)(B) provides that a statement is not hearsay if the statement is offered against a party and is "a statement of which the party has manifested an adoption or belief in its truth."

Cases and Authorities

See *United States v. Robinson*, 275 F.3d 371, 383 (4th Cir. 2001)(adoption of statement of another person may be by words, conduct or *silence* on the part of the adopting party; if a party hears blameworthy or accusatory words uttered in his presence and he disagrees with the incriminating statements, he should have made his disagreement known); *United States v. Henke*, 222 F.3d 633, 642 (9th Cir. 2000)(adoption by failure to respond).

While many adoptive admissions arise from failure to respond to oral accusations, some emanate from a party's refusal to respond to a written accusation. *Hellenic Lines Ltd. v. Gulf Oil Corp.*, 340 F.2d 398, 401 (2d Cir. 1965)(failure of party to respond to a letter constituted admission by silence, where circumstances reasonably called for a response).

In addition to admissions by silence, a party can affirmatively adopt another's words by agreeing with the speaker. *United States v. Jinadu*, 98 F.3d 239, 245 (6th Cir. 1996)(accused answered accusation "you knew it was China White heroin?" with a "yes").

Comment

Adoptive admissions can be expressed or implied. The transcript example in this section is of the latter kind, and admissions by silence can form an important part of a litigant's proof in either civil or criminal cases. The accusation, in order to create an adoptive admission against the charged party, must be made in a situation where it would be natural to deny the accusation. Otherwise, no admission is made. For example, if someone screams at one of the drivers involved in an auto wreck while the driver is kneeling down beside an injured person trying to stop the bleeding, he need not reply. No adoptive admission is created against the driver.

In criminal cases, adoptive admissions—also called tacit admissions—are limited to pre-*Miranda* situations. For details on *Miranda*, see the *Admissions* entry in this text as well as *Confessions*, infra; see also *Miranda v. Arizona*, 384 U.S. 436, 86 S.Ct. 1602, 16 L.Ed.2d 694 (1966). Admissions by silence in criminal cases, see discussion in *Doyle v. Ohio*, 426 U.S. 610, 617–19, 96 S.Ct. 2240, 2244–45, 49 L.Ed.2d 91, 98 (1976)(after defendant has been warned about his right to silence by means of <u>Miranda</u> warnings, impeachment by use of the accused's silence after he invoked his rights is unconstitutional); *Jenkins v. Anderson*, 447 U.S. 231, 100 S.Ct. 2124, 2130, 65 L.Ed.2d 86, 96 (1980)(impeachment by means of an accused's prearrest silence does not violate Fourteenth Amendment); *Fletcher v. Weir*, 455 U.S. 603, 605–07, 102 S.Ct. 1309, 1311–12, 71 L.Ed.2d 490, 493–94 (1982)(deals with situation between *Doyle* and *Jenkins*; holds that prosecutor may use postarrest silence for impeachment if defendant had not yet been given *Miranda* warnings).

For a good example of prearrest silence which stands as an adoptive admission, see *United States v. Kehoe*, 310 F.3d 579, 590–91 (8th Cir. 2002)(holding defendant adopted statements made by his accomplice when accomplice recounted details of defendant's participation in murder to a witness; the witness testified that the defendant was present when statements were made, there was nothing to suggest defendant did not understand statements, and defendant actively participated in conversation and did not deny or contradict accomplice's statements).

Age

Elements

To prove the age of a living or deceased person, the proponent of the evidence may establish age by: 1) certified copy of birth certificate; 2) birth record maintained by a public agency or by a hospital; 3) declarations of close relatives regarding the age of a family member; and 4) if a live witness is on the stand and testifying, her declarations as to her own age are competent.

Direct Examination

Q. Mr. Jones, how old are you?

A. I am 37 years old.

Q. Are your parents alive?

A. No, they are both dead.

Q. Prior to their deaths, did you have any conversations with them about your age?

A. They made numerous statements to me on that subject, usually on events such as my birthdays and when I got my driver's license.

Q. What did they say?

Objection by Opponent: Hearsay.

Response by Proponent: Reliable hearsay is admissible to help establish date of birth, your honor.

Court: Overruled.

A. They confirmed that I was born on ...., 19.. (witness gives date of birth).

Rule Reference

Federal Rule of Evidence 804(b)(4), pertaining to statements of personal or family history, provides an exception to the hearsay rule with respect to "(A)[a] statement concerning the declarant's own birth, adoption, marriage, divorce, legitimacy, relationship by blood, adoption, or marriage, ancestry or other similar fact of personal or family history, even though declarant had no means of acquiring personal knowledge of the matter stated; or (B) a statement concerning the foregoing matters, and death also, of another person, if the declarant was related to the other by blood, adoption, or marriage or was so intimately associated with the other's family as to be likely to have accurate information concerning the matter declared."

Cases and Authorities

Age is sometimes the object of testimony in child sex abuse prosecutions, and in one case the statements of the victim's mother about her daughter's birthday was admissible under the hearsay exception as to pedigree. *State v. Mitchell*, 568 N.W.2d 493, 500 (Iowa 1997). In civil actions, disputes as to age also play a role. For example, a claimant for retirement benefits may need to prove his age. A landowner in a property dispute proved he was 70 years old by his birth certificate in *Lillianfeld v. Lichtenstein*, 181 Misc.2d 571, 694 N.Y.S.2d 600 (Sup. Ct. 1999).

Two distinct scenarios may confront the trial lawyer. In the first, her client whose age is in dispute may be alive and available to testify. The person can simply be put on the witness stand to state his age. In most cases, this will suffice to establish a person's age. However, in cases involving a serious age dispute this may not be sufficient. Much depends upon the attitude of the court and the intensity of the debate over the person's age. In hotly contested situations, other forms of supportive proof will be called for.

The "pedigree exception" to the hearsay rule may be a source of assistance, embraced in Rule 804(B)(4), Fed. R. Evid. Under the Rule, comments made in earlier days by currently unavailable family members during their lifetime regarding a person's age may be quoted in court. A wide range of documentary evidence may also be summoned in order to reinforce the witness' own age testimony.

Occasionally a lawyer is attempting to establish the date of birth of a deceased person. Here, secondary proof will be essential.

Comment

In addition to Federal Evidence Rule 804(b)(4), there is another rule which can play a role in establishing one's age. Rule 803(9) provides admissibility for records of vital statistics. The Rule admits into evidence "[r]ecords or data compilations, in any form, of births, fetal deaths, deaths, or marriages, if the report thereof was made to a public office pursuant to requirements of law." A birth record may be advanced under this rule.

This section of the text notes that extrajudicial declarations by family members may be reported in court under the pedigree exception to the hearsay rule. Also, entries in family Bibles respecting such matters as births, deaths, and marriages of members of the family are competent evidence on these issues. Baptismal, school, church or hospital records as well as certified copies of birth certificates are additional methods of proving age. Finally, the ancient documents rule may be of assistance when authenticating old papers which bear upon the age issue. See *Ancient Documents*, infra.

Agent Admissions

Elements

When an employee of a party makes a declaration, the declaration can bind the principal where the opponent establishes these elements: 1) at a prior time a party's agent made a statement to or in the presence of a witness who identifies the employee as the author of the remark; 2) the trial witness is called by one party (party A) and the declaration was uttered by an agent of the opposing party (party B); 3) the agent was an employee of party B when the statement was made; and 4) the declaration concerned a matter within the scope of the declarant's agency or employment.

Direct Examination

Q. (by plaintiff's attorney in a products liability case) Mr. Baldus, what is your position with Independent Auto Design, Inc.?

A. Chief design engineer.

Q. In that capacity, have you had occasion to discuss auto design considerations with an officer of the defendant, Marathon Motors?

A. Yes. Their vice-president for product development was in regular contact with me over the last two years regarding design of the fuel system on the Marathon Marauder. The vice-president is Bixby Swanson.

Q. Did you discuss the design of the Marauder which caused the burn injuries in this case?

A. Yes, on two occasions.

Q. Where did those conversations take place?

A. In his office at Marathon.

Q. When did they occur?

A. Last July 19 and 23.

Q. What did Mr. Swanson say?

Objection by Defense: Hearsay, your honor.

Plaintiff's Attorney: Admission by the defendant's agent, your honor.

Court: Overruled.

Q. (by plaintiff's attorney) Will you please answer the question, Mr. Baldus?

A. The vice-president said "That tank is dangerous, sure, but it just costs too much to change things now."

Rule Reference

Federal Rule of Evidence 801(d)(2)(D) provides that a statement is not hearsay if it is offered against a party and is "a statement by the party's agent or servant concerning a matter within the scope of the agency or employment, made during the existence of the relationship."

Cases and Authorities

See *Abuan v. Level 3 Communications, Inc.*, 353 F.3d 1158, 1170–72 (10th Cir. 2003)(admitting testimony by plaintiff's witness that corporation vice president who supervised plaintiff stated during vice president's going-away luncheon that he was resigning in part due to employer's unethical treatment of plaintiff; statements by vice president were made by a corporation's agent who was speaking about a matter within scope of the officer's employment, during existence of employment relationship). In *Sea-Land Service, Inc. v Lozen Int'l, LLC*, 285

F.3d 808, 821–22 (9th Cir. 2002) the district court abused its discretion when it excluded an e-mail which contained an agent admission. The case of *Stalbosky v Belew*, 205 F.3d 890, 895 (6th Cir. 2000) involved statements by a semi-retired agent, which statements should have been held against the employer. See also *Aliotta v. National R.R. Passenger Corp.*, 315 F.3d 756, 763–64 (7th Cir. 2003), where statements of defendant's manager were admissible under the hearsay rule as agent admissions. Although the hearsay rule was satisfied, says this case, such declarations might be subject to other, different objections.

One set of agents whose admissions will not bind the employer are police who made admissions in criminal cases, where the defense seeks to use the admissions against the state. As observed in A. Poulin, Party Admissions in Criminal Cases: Should the Government Have to Eat Its Words?, 87 Minn. L. Rev. 401 (2002), evidence law gives the government an advantage in criminal trials because the prosecution is not responsible for prior statements made by agents acting or speaking for the government. Many courts have held that in criminal cases the statements of government agents are not admissible over hearsay objections as party admissions. The defendant is often precluded from even informing the jury of helpful statements made by government agents. Professor Poulin criticizes the fairness of this approach in her article.

Comment

An employee makes binding admissions against his employer when he speaks about a matter within the agent's authority. For example, a company may be sued for negligence in connection with an accident involving one of its trucks. If the employee who drove the truck for the defendant company makes declarations about the nature of his driving and how he caused the accident, these declarations by the driver are admissible against the employer when offered by the plaintiff.

When executives of a company make admissions, the general executive authority of the company official sufficiently qualifies the official to author binding admissions. Binding agency admissions, see *Crawford v. Garnier*, 719 F.2d 1317, 1324 (7th Cir. 1983); 12A Federal Procedure L. Ed. Evidence § 33:377. Proof of Agency, see 14 Am. Jur. Proof of Facts 2d 483.

For admissions which contain references to insurance, see the entry in this text for *Insurance Information*.

Ancient Documents

Elements

In order for counsel to introduce an old writing under this hearsay exception, she must demonstrate that 1) it was discovered in a location where a person would reasonably believe such a document might be found; 2) the condition of the document suggests that erasures or alterations have not been made in its terms or contents; and 3) the document is at least 20 years old.

Direct Examination

Q. Mr. Smith, were you at one time associated with William X. Herndon in the firm of Smith and Herndon?

A. Yes.

Q. When?

A. 1980 to 1999. Will Herndon died in 1999.

Q. I show you plaintiff's exhibit A for identification, which purports to be a deed from Walter Landers to Geno Z. Crawford, dated January 15, 1982. Have you seen this document before?

A. Yes. I was in the office at the time it was drafted.

Q. Are you familiar with attorney Herndon's handwriting?

A. Yes. We exchanged letters and notes many times over the years.

Q. Do you recognize the handwriting which appears in the blank places on the deed?

A. Yes. It is that of attorney Herndon, who drew the deed.

Q. Where has it been since that time?

A. Our office file. The grantor had a great deal of confidence in Mr. Herndon.

To the Court: Your honor, I offer in evidence plaintiff's exhibit A, the deed bearing date of January 15, 1982.

Court: Received.

Rule References

Federal Rule of Evidence 803(16) provides for the admissibility of statements in a document in existence twenty years or more, the authenticity of which is established.

Federal Evidence Rule 901(b)(8) provides for the authentication of ancient documents or data compilation by means of evidence that a document or data compilation, in any form, (A) is in such condition as to create no suspicion concerning its authenticity, (B) was in a place where it, if authentic, would likely be, and (C) has been in existence 20 years or more at the time it is offered.

Cases and Authorities

A variety of documents have been admitted under this rule. World War II records were introduced in *United States v. Stelmokas*, 100 F.3d 302, 311–13 (3d Cir. 1996)(documents from Lithuanian archives demonstrated employment activities of defendant during World War II). Witness statements dating to 1945 were admitted into evidence in *United States v. Hajda*, 135 F.3d 439, 444 (7th Cir. 1998)(documents over 20 years old and properly authenticated satisfy Rule 803(16)). In *Kalamazoo River Study Group v. Menasha Corp.*, 228 F.3d 648, 662 (6th Cir. 2000), a document was excluded. The document was an alleged EPA report, which was rejected when the sponsoring witness could not state with certainty that it was prepared by the EPA or why it was in the files of a state agency. Old newspaper articles introduced, see *Dallas County v. Commercial Union Assurance Co.*, 286 F.2d 388 (5th Cir. 1961).

Comment

Written instruments and documents of many kinds purporting to be 20 years old or more, if relevant, are admissible. However, a showing should be made that they are regular on their face and came from proper custody. It is for the court to determine whether enough proof of a document's age and genuineness has been offered to allow its admission into evidence. Under the common law this age was 30 years. The federal rule shortened this to 20 years.

See *Astra Aktiebolag v. Andrx Pharms., Inc.*, 222 F.Supp.2d 423, 574–75 (S.D.N.Y. 2002)(finding documents sufficiently authenticated on showing that originals of documents were found where they would most likely be (defendant's headquarters and laboratory), dates on originals along with testimony of defendant's U.S. distributor established documents were more than twenty years old, and documents appeared to have been read a number of times, with pages wrinkled, torn, folded, and yellowed).

Where handwriting or signatures appear on the writing, it is sometimes helpful for counsel to provide handwriting authentication along with proof of the document's age. The trial proof in this section of the text combines these concepts. For more on establishing identity of handwriting, in this text see *Handwriting*, infra.

Best and Secondary Evidence

Elements

When producing secondary evidence of a writing in cases where the terms of the original are disputed and the original is unproduced, the following points need to be established: 1) the original of the contract or other writing is not in the possession of the tendering party; 2) either its whereabouts are unknown or it has been destroyed or stolen, or it is beyond the reach of the subpoena process; 3) in rare cases, the opponent has the document and refuses to produce it in response to a motion to produce or other appropriate request; 4) in no event is the absence or destruction of the original a result of bad conduct by the party who offers secondary evidence.

Direct Examination

Q. (by Plaintiff's Attorney) Mr. Plaintiff, you are suing in this case for lost profits?

A. Yes. The car accident which is the subject of this lawsuit prevented me from performing a lucrative contract with a business associate, Mr. Garwood Burns.

Q. After the contracts were executed by you and Mr. Burns, what happened?

A. There were a couple of unsigned copies which had been made on the copying machine. I took one of these and Mr. Burns took the other. Then he left on his flight to his home in Anchorage.

Q. What happened to your signed contract?

A. I took mine on a business trip to look it over and my briefcase was stolen. The contract was in it.

Q. You indicated that there were two signed originals. Did you try to get the other original from Mr. Burns?

A. Yes. He was apparently angry because I couldn't follow through on the contract as a result of my accident, and he refused to send me his original of the contract.

Q. I hand you plaintiff's exhibit 1 for identification and ask if you can identify it?

A. Yes, this is a copy of the contract. It is one of the copies that was made on the day the contracts were signed. Of course, we did not sign all the copies.

Q. Does it accurately reflect the terms of the original?

A. Yes. There are only a few differences. The originals contained the signature of Mr. Burns and myself. Also, the date we signed the contracts was entered in ink on both originals. Except for those two items, this copy—this exhibit—duplicates the originals exactly. It accurately reflects the amount of profits I lost on this deal because my work was foreclosed by the accident.

To the Court: Plaintiff's exhibit 1 for identification, the copy of the plaintiff's contract, is offered into evidence as plaintiff's exhibit 1.

Court: Received.

Rule Reference

Federal Evidence Rule 1004. Admissibility of Other Evidence of Contents. The original is not required, and other evidence of the contents of a writing, recording, or photograph is admissible if—

(1) Originals lost or destroyed. All originals are lost or have been destroyed, unless the proponent lost or destroyed them in bad faith; or

(2) Original not obtainable. No original can be obtained by any available judicial process or procedure; or

(3) Original in possession of opponent. At a time when an original was under the control of the party against whom offered, that party was put on notice, by the pleadings or otherwise, that the contents would be a subject of proof at the hearing, and that party does not produce the original at the hearing; or

(4) Collateral matters. The writing, recording, or photograph is not closely related to a controlling issue.

Cases and Authorities

The ability to prove the content or terms of a document or writing by substitute or secondary evidence can save a case. See, e.g., *Burt Rigid Box, Inc. v. Travelers Prop. Cas. Corp.*, 302 F.3d 83, 91–93 (2d Cir. 2002)(applying rule in context of lost insurance policy, allowing insured to rely on secondary evidence to prove existence and terms of insurance policy where there was diligent but unsuccessful search and inquiry for missing policy). The proponent of the secondary evidence must show that he did not intentionally cause the loss of the original. See *Paul Revere Variable Annuity Ins. Co. v. Zang*, 81 F.Supp.2d 227, 230 (D. Mass. 2000)(court admitted affidavits showing existence of arbitration agreement when the original agreement was lost or destroyed without bad faith).

Comment

The original is not required, and other evidence of the contents of a writing, recording, or photograph is admissible, if the proponent excuses nonproduction of the original. Nonproduction of the original may be excused by a showing that all originals are lost or have been destroyed, unless the proponent lost or destroyed them in bad faith. Other recognized excuses for nonproduction of the original include situations where no original can be obtained by available judicial process, the opposing party has the original and will not produce it, or the writing is not closely related to a controlling issue in the case.

The contract referred to in the foregoing trial proof relates to one of the controlling issues in the case, monies lost as a result of an automobile accident which rendered one of the contracting parties unable to perform. Secondary evidence is admissible where the primary evidence is shown to be outside the jurisdiction, and the court is powerless to compel attendance of the party having present custody of the evidence or the evidence itself. As a preliminary to the introduction of a copy, it must usually be shown that the copy is an authentic reflection of the original. Introduction of secondary evidence, see 35 Am. Jur. Proof of Facts 2d 147. Related matters, see *Summaries*, infra, for situations where secondary evidence may become admissible where it is impracticable to admit the primary evidence in court because of the volume of the original writings.

Bias

Elements

To impeach a witness with a showing of bias, the following elements frequently mark the impeachment process: 1) an opposing witness has made statements or engaged in conduct prior to the trial which discloses his prejudice against your client, or in favor of the side which calls him to the stand; 2) your cross-examination of the defendant identifies the nature of the bias and, where the witness has expressed it in statements, when and to whom those were made; 3) if you decide to call an extrinsic witness to help prove the bias, your examination of the extrinsic witness will also identify the nature of the bias and the manner in which it was expressed.

Cross-Examination

In an automobile negligence case, the following line of questions might be used against a witness who is called by the plaintiff to help prove that the plaintiff entered an intersection in compliance with the green light. The defense is cross-examining.

Q. (by Defense Attorney) Mr. Gardner, you said on direct a few moments ago that my client ran the red light. Do you recall when I came to your apartment in July?

A. Could be.

Q. Didn't you refuse to speak with me?

A. Yeah. I didn't want to talk to you.

Q. But you did cooperate with the plaintiff?

A. **(antagonistic)** So what!

Defense: That's all.

Cases and Authorities

See *United States v. Abel*, 469 U.S. 45, 105 S.Ct. 465, 83 L.Ed.2d 450 (1984); *United States v. Crouch*, 478 F.Supp. 867, 871 (E.D. Cal. 1979)(holding that a witness' refusal to talk to a party's attorney may be brought out in trial as evidence of the witness' possible bias). A showing of financial interest in the outcome of the litigation on the part of the witness is a good way to prove bias. So is a business relationship, or former business relationship between the witness and one of the parties. See *United States v. Boone*, 279 F.3d 163, 175 (3d Cir. 2002) (allowing limited cross-examination into whether defense witness had once sold drugs for defendant charged with drug conspiracy, to show bias). Sometimes otherwise inadmissible facts may be asked about if they demonstrate bias. See *Pecoraro v. Walls*, 286 F.3d 439, 445 (7th Cir. 2002) (under law, defendant may inquire into whether witness has been arrested where it would reasonably show bias).

Comment

Where information exists which demonstrates that a witness is biased in favor of your adversary, dislikes your client, or otherwise is interested in the outcome of the case, proof of bias can be made by cross-examining the biased witness, calling another witness to prove bias, or both. With respect to the specific demonstration of potential bias contained in the factual scenario featured here, see *Crouch*, 478 F.Supp. at 871 . Bias may be shown by inquiry into family ties between the witness and one of the parties, romantic involvement, financial ties, prior business or criminal association with one of the parties, and the like. The latitude allowed an attorney to cross-examine about bias is very broad.

In the case of an expert witness, cross-examination for bias can take a number of forms. The fixed point of view of a doctor may be an apt object for a cross-examiner's attention. In a malpractice case, plaintiff's counsel may ask:

Q. Doctor Jansen, how many times have testified in medical malpractice litigation?

A. Fourteen times.

Q. Did you, on any of those occasions, ever testify that a doctor was guilty of malpractice?

A. I can't recall that I have.

Another source of bias examination is to ask the expert about his or her fees. Those earned in the present case are open to disclosure. Fees earned in prior cases may also be exposed. See the *Fees* entry in this text.

Bias examination, see 58 Am. Jur. Proof of Facts 3d 395.

Bills [Reasonableness]

Elements

When it comes to collecting monetary damages, a lawyer is frequently called upon to prove up her client's bills and expenses. When she proceeds to do so, these elements usually must be demonstrated: 1) services were rendered which are memorialized in a statement or a bill; 2) in the absence of a stipulation as to reasonableness of the charges contained in the bill, a person qualified to do so affirms the reasonableness of the amounts.

Direct Examination

In a personal injury case, the plaintiff's physician is frequently called upon to authenticate his medical charges.

Q. Dr. Crump, I show you plaintiff's exhibit 9, purporting to be a statement of medical services rendered plaintiff from July 30, 2004 to January 1, 2005. Do you recognize this document?

A. Yes, I was the plaintiff's attending physician and submitted that bill.

Q. How long have you practiced medicine in this city?

A. Eight years.

Q. Are you acquainted with the customary reasonable charges for medical services in this city?

A. Yes.

Q. Do you have an opinion, based on your experience in the practice of medicine, as to whether the amount of the bill for medical services rendered to the plaintiff was reasonable?

A. Yes.

Q. What is that opinion?

A. That such amount is reasonable.

Q. Was the course of treatment covered by the bill necessitated by the accident in this case?

A. Yes.

Rule Reference

Federal Evidence Rule 901. Requirement of Authentication or Identification.

(a) General provision. The requirement of authentication or identification as a condition precedent to admissibility is satisfied by evidence sufficient to support a finding that the matter in question is what its proponent claims.

Cases and Authorities

See *Cameron v. United States*, 135 F.Supp.2d 775, 779–80 (S.D. Tex. 2001)(doctor familiar with charges for certain medical services in the area allowed to testify as to the reasonableness of plaintiff's medical bills). Bills other than those for medical services often require legitimation as well. See *Kallman v. Radioshack Corp.*, 315 F.3d 731, 742 (7th Cir. 2002)(finding strong evidence of commercial reasonableness where landlord incurred and paid bill for legal services in breach of commercial lease litigation against guarantor, noting this was all that indemnity clause required).

Comment

Where both sides are presenting bills, it is often customary for the lawyers for each party to agree on the reasonableness of the other side's bills. This, of course, eliminates the need to call a sponsoring witness to support the reasonableness of the charges reflected on the bills. In medical injury cases, a limited stipulation may be feasible. Under it, the defense lawyer agrees to the reasonableness of amounts for various services stated on the plaintiff's bill; however, the defense does not agree that all of the medical services referenced on the bill were required on account of the accident, explosion, medical malpractice or other episode which is the subject of the litigation.

On proving charges and bills, see 4 Am. Jur. Proof of Facts 71, at 119. In addition to bills for medical services, a bill for nursing services may need to be proved up. Transcripts for doing so appear in R. Carlson, Successful Techniques for Civil Trials 2d § 3:38 (1992); 4 Am. Jur. Proof of Facts 71, at 120–121. Bills for repairs of automobiles and their reasonableness are illustrated in Carlson, supra at § 3:37. The following is an illustration of such proof. After establishing that the witness is an experienced auto body repair specialist who works at Ace Auto Repair, the plaintiff's attorney asks:

Q. Did you repair the plaintiff's car?

A. Yes.

Q. Will you please describe the damage you repaired?

A. Yes. The grille of the 2004 Chrysler 300M owned by the plaintiff, Mr. Jacobs, had extensive damage across the front of the grille. It was cracked and had to be replaced. The hood of the car was also dented, but I was able to straighten it and smooth it out and repaint it. I did the same for the left front fender.

Q. I show you this bill marked plaintiff's exhibit 10. What is it?

A. That is the bill submitted by Ace for the repairs I have described.

Q. Who prepared this bill?

A. I did.

Q. Based upon your training and experience as an auto repairman and body shop supervisor, are you acquainted with the fair, reasonable and customary charge for parts, work and labor in installing a grille on a 2004 Chrysler, and for straightening dents in the hood and fender and repainting?

A. Yes.

Q. What is it?

A. $3,170.50 (this figure coincides with the amount of the bill).

Business Records

Elements

When financial or other routinely kept records are relevant to a case, calling to the stand someone from the business or professional office which generated the records set the stage for document introduction. These elements should be covered with the witness: 1) records of regularly conducted activity are authenticated through the author of the record, or the custodian, or other qualified witness; 2) the witness affirms the manner of preparation of the record, and often commercial records are prepared from information derived from people with firsthand knowledge of the events recorded and a business duty to report them; 3) the regularity of preparation in a timely fashion is established; 4) the business report was routinely prepared for the regular conduct of the business or profession and the record was not specially prepared for this litigation.

Direct Examination

Medical records qualify as business records under the rules of evidence. An M.D., for example, can be an authenticating witness for her own records in a personal injury case.

Q. Doctor, how many visits has the plaintiff made to your office for diagnosis and treatment since the accident?

A. Sixteen.

Q. As a matter of office practice, do you prepare a diagnostic report for your files?

A. Yes. In the case of patients whom I will be treating for extended periods, I prepare such a report. The original goes in the patient's file in my office.

Q. When do you do this?

A. I dictate such a report shortly after my examinations and tests provide sufficient data to reach some firm conclusions. In this case, the report was prepared after the third office visit.

Q. How routinely is this done?

A. I do this with every case that looks like it will require extended treatment, and it has nothing to do with whether a case is in, or is likely to go to, litigation.

Q. I hand you what has been marked Plaintiff's Exhibit 2. **(Counsel hands paper to witness)** What is it?

A. The report I referred to.

Plaintiff's Attorney: I offer the report as a business record. I will not take the time to review all the doctor's test results and findings now, but I will want to refer to portions of this record in my argument later, as evidence in the case.

Defense Attorney: Objection, hearsay.

Court: Overruled.

Rule References

Federal Evidence Rule 803(6). Records of regularly conducted activity. A memorandum, report, record, or data compilation, in any form, of acts, events, conditions, opinions, or diagnoses, made at or near the time by, or from information transmitted by, a person with knowledge, if kept in the course of a regularly conducted business activity, and if it was the regular practice of that business activity to make the memorandum, report, record, or data compilation, all as shown by the testimony of the custodian or other qualified witness or by certification that complies with Rule 902(11), Rule 902(12), or a statute permitting certification, unless the source of information or the method or circumstances of preparation indicate lack of trustworthiness. The term "business" as used in this paragraph includes business, institution, association, profession, occupation, and calling of every kind, whether or not conducted for profit.

Federal Evidence Rule 902(11). Certified domestic records of regularly conducted activity. The original or a duplicate of a domestic record of regularly conducted activity that would be admissible under Rule 803(6) if accompanied by a written declaration of its custodian or other qualified person, in a manner complying with any Act of Congress or rule prescribed by the Supreme Court pursuant to statutory authority, certifying that the record—

(A) was made at or near the time of the occurrence of the matters set forth by, or from information transmitted by, a person with knowledge of those matters;

(B) was kept in the course of the regularly conducted activity; and

(C) was made by the regularly conducted activity as a regular practice.

A party intending to offer a record into evidence under this paragraph must provide written notice of that intention to all adverse parties, and must make the record and declaration available for inspection sufficiently in advance of their offer into evidence to provide an adverse party with a fair opportunity to challenge them.

Federal Evidence Rule 902(12). Certified foreign records of regularly conducted activity. In a civil case, the original or a duplicate of a foreign record of regularly conducted activity that would be admissible under Rule 803(6) if accompanied by a written declaration by its custodian or other qualified person certifying that the record—

(A) was made at or near the time of the occurrence of the matters set forth by, or from information transmitted by, a person with knowledge of those matters;

(B) was kept in the course of the regularly conducted activity; and

(C) was made by the regularly conducted activity as a regular practice.

The declaration must be signed in a manner that, if falsely made, would subject the maker to criminal penalty under the laws of the country where the declaration is signed. A party intending to offer a record into evidence under this paragraph must provide written notice of that intention to all adverse parties, and must make the record and declaration available for inspection sufficiently in advance of their offer into evidence to provide an adverse party with a fair opportunity to challenge them.

Cases and Authorities

Lack of an appropriate authenticating witness can cause a breakdown in the production of business record proof. See *Shu-Hui Chen v. Bouchard,* 347 F.3d 1299, 1308 (Fed. Cir. 2003) (finding non-testifying researcher's notebooks not within business records hearsay exception where it was not established that notebooks were actually those of said author, and no evidence established the employer's policies regarding maintenance of laboratory notebooks; proponent presented no testimony from "custodian or other qualified witness" that notebooks were "records of regularly conducted activity"); *United States v. Dickerson,* 248 F.3d 1036, 1048 (11th Cir. 2001) (district court erred in admitting hotel records to establish dates a witness was in town, but error was harmless; the Government presented no "custodian or other qualified witness" from the hotel, so reliability of records not established).

The theory behind the introduction of business records is contained in *Clark v. City of Los Angeles,* 650 F.2d 1033, 1037

(9th Cir. 1981). Under this case, admissible business records must be made pursuant to established company procedures, and relied upon by the business in the performance of its functions. According to *Clark*, a diary should not have been admitted as a business record.

The *Clark* case also held that expressions of opinion in business records are admissible only if the opinion is given by one with the required competence. 650 F.2d at 1037. The issue of opinions in business records has generated litigation. Federal Rule 803(6) embraces business records laced with opinions. Such was not the approach of the common law—the common law held that business records were limited to financial data and factual information only—and a number of states continue to follow this view. See, e.g., R. Carlson, Trial Handbook for Georgia Lawyers § 25:13 (3d ed. 2003)("if the writing contains diagnostic opinions or conclusions it cannot be admitted over objection")(citing cases). Even jurisdictions which have adopted evidence codes based upon the Federal Rules of Evidence have sometimes not enacted the portion of Fed. R. Evid. 803(6) which allows introduction of records containing "opinions or diagnoses." See, e.g., Rule 803(6), Oh. R. Evid.

Occasionally it becomes opportune for a party to demonstrate nonexistence of a fact by its absence from a routinely prepared record. The federal rules carefully carve out a hearsay exception for this contingency. Rule 803(7) provides as follows: "Evidence that a matter is not included in the memoranda reports, records, or data compilations, in any form, kept in accordance with the provisions of paragraph 803(6), to prove the nonoccurrence or nonexistence of the matter, if the matter was of a kind of which a memorandum, report, record, or data compilation was regularly made and preserved, unless the sources of information or other circumstances indicate lack of trustworthiness."

Comment

The business records exception to the hearsay rule has been expanded from strictly commercial books of account to encompass hospital, doctor, and other records. Thus, the federal rule extends admissibility to opinions or diagnoses contained in regularly prepared records. However, many times the lawyer will authenticate that which was traditional under the rule, a company's book of accounts or electronically recorded record of financial accounts. Interrogation of the custodian of the company records should establish these points:

(1) The record, report, or business entry was prepared in the regular and ordinary course of business.

(2) The memo, report or record was prepared by a business employee.

(3) The person in the line of company employees with first-hand knowledge of the reported transaction had a business duty to report or record the relevant information.

(4) The company record was made at or near the time when the transaction took place, which transaction is the subject of the business record.

(5) The business item was recorded either in a written documentary form, or by means of computer, and the business relied on such documents or computer records for its regular operation.

(6) The authenticating witness must be the keeper of the records, or a company officer familiar with the company's record keeping routines.

This sort of proof avoids the "record made solely for litigation" objection. *Palmer v. Hoffman*, 318 U.S. 109, 63 S.Ct. 477, 87 L.Ed. 645 (1943); *Certain Underwriters at Lloyd's London v. Sinkovich*, 232 F.3d 200 (4th Cir. 2000). When records produced by electronic means are offered, a printout is a common method of presentation. Other entries in this text related to business records include *Best Evidence* and *Computer Records*.

Proof of Facts references, see 14 Am. Jur. Proof of Facts 2d 173; 34 Am. Jur. Proof of Facts 2d 509; 38 Am. Jur. Proof of Facts 2d 145.

Self-Authentication Amendments

In December, 2000, the Federal Evidence Rules were amended in a manner to ease introduction of business records. The amendment is explained in Gibbons, A Student's Guide to Trial Objections 9–10 (2003).

The business records of American companies are now admissible in civil and criminal cases without the need to call a witness if: (1) accompanied by a written declaration by the custodian or other qualified person that the records (a) were made at our near the time of the occurrence at issue or from information transmitted by a person with knowledge, (b) were kept in the ordinary course of business, (c) were created by the business as a regular practice; and (2) the offering party gives notice of intended use to all adverse parties and opportunity to inspect the records and the declaration so as to provide a fair opportunity to challenge them. Rule 902(11).

The same procedure applies to foreign business records to be used in civil cases. Rule 902(12). A statute, 18 U.S.C.A. § 3505, already provides a similar route to admissibility in criminal cases and has withstood Confrontation Clause challenges. *United States v. Garcia Abrego*, 141 F.3d 142, 178–79 (5th Cir. 1998)(collecting cases).

Integrated Records Doctrine

Sometimes an officer of Company A is asked to authenticate the records of Company B. This comes up in the following manner. Company B's reports or records are routinely routed to Company A for use by the latter company, and they are relied upon by Company A as it conducts its daily business. Further, the records of Company B are integrated into the files of Company A. Under these circumstances, an officer of Company A can authenticate the records of Company B in the same manner as if they had been prepared by employees of Company A. See *MRT Construction v. Hardrives, Inc.,* 158 F.3d 478 (9th Cir. 1998) (records derived from others are admissible when the business which receives them keeps them in the regular course of business, relies upon them, and has a substantial interest in their accuracy); *United States v. Childs,* 5 F.3d 1328 (9th Cir. 1993) (outside documents prepared by third parties and integrated into the records of an auto dealership were properly introduced based upon testimony by the dealership's employee that such records were maintained at the dealership in the regular course of business and relied upon; not fatal to introduction that dealer did not make the record).

Character and Reputation: Truthfulness

Elements

This entry relates to reputation proof on the issue of *credibility*. Sometimes it is helpful, after your witness or party has been attacked, to call a character witness to support the attacked person. In examining such a character witness, the following points need to be established: 1) the reputation testimony which is sought from the witness must relate to the supported person's reputation for telling the truth, which reputation the supported person enjoys in the neighborhood where he lives or in his school, place of employment, business, or profession; 2) some association between the character witness and the supported witness or party should be shown; 3) frequent contact by the character witness with individuals who know the supported person; establish the fact that the trial witness has heard neighborhood or community discussions concerning the other person.

Direct Examination

In the following example, the plaintiff Gary Coddington has already testified in his business dispute with Cannon Parcel Services over misdelivery of important packages. In the hypothetical case of Coddington v. Cannon Parcel Services, plaintiff Coddington was vigorously cross-examined. The plaintiff's attorney now calls a friend of the plaintiff to the stand to reflect upon Coddington's character.

Q. Mr. Jones, do you know Gary Coddington, the plaintiff in this case?

A. Yes.

Q. How long have you known him?

A. Ever since I moved into my current house. He was already living next door. So that's about four years.

Q. Are you related by blood or marriage to the plaintiff?

A. No.

Q. Do you know his occupation?

A. Yes.

Q. What is it?

A. He owns his own small company. Gary is President and plant superintendent for Coddington Manufacturing Company.

Q. During the time that you lived in the neighborhood with the plaintiff, have you had occasion to speak with others in the community about him?

A. I certainly have. Our community is a friendly one.

Q. Have you talked to other neighbors about the plaintiff?

A. Yes, several times.

Q. Can you tell us approximately how many times?

A. At least 30 times.

Q. About how many different persons have spoken with you concerning the plaintiff, conversations that would have touched on his character for truthfulness or his reputation for honesty?

A. Twelve to fifteen people, I would estimate.

Q. Does the plaintiff have a reputation for truth and veracity in the community where you and he live?

A. Yes.

Q. What is that reputation?

A. It is very good. Gary is known as a truthful and honest person. [In some states the direct examiner is allowed to ask: "Would you believe him under oath?"]

Rule References

Federal Evidence Rule 608(a). Opinion and reputation evidence of character. The credibility of a witness may be attacked or supported by evidence in the form of opinion or reputation, but subject to these limitations: (1) The evidence may refer only to character for truthfulness or untruthfulness, and (2) evidence of truthful character is admissible only after the character of the witness for truthfulness has been attacked by opinion or reputation evidence or otherwise.

Federal Evidence Rule 803(21) provides a hearsay exception for reputation proof, allowing "[r]eputation of a person's character among associates or in the community."

Cases and Authorities

A needed predicate to introducing "good character" evidence is the requirement that the supported witness be first attacked. See *United States v. Universal Rehabilitation Services, Inc.*, 205 F.3d 657, 680 (3d Cir. 2000)(character evidence in support of truthfulness is admissible only after witness' credibility has been attacked). While such an attack usually comes (if at all) during cross-examination, sometimes it occurs earlier. See *Renda v. King*, 347 F.3d 550, 554–56 (3d Cir. 2003)(holding that arrestee's opening statement suggesting corruption by officer went beyond alleging bias and was indirect attack on witness' character for truthfulness, opening door for evidence of witness's good character for truthfulness).

As noted, in some jurisdictions the reputation witness may go beyond simply community knowledge and can assert that the witness would believe the other party under oath. See OCGA § 24–9–81 (Georgia).

Proof of another person's bad character for truthfulness may also be made. Whether examining a character witness under Federal Evidence Rule 608 regarding another individual's good or bad character, counsel needs to take care to concentrate her questions on the truthfulness or untruthfulness of the other party.

Comment

See Rule 608(a), Federal Rules of Evidence, which authorizes proof of character by personal opinion or by reputation. Often the first instances of character proof in a trial provide a favorable view of the supported party. A supportive character witness is called. After his direct, he is cross-examined. On cross-examination of a Rule 608 reputation witness, inquiry can be made about specific relevant instances of dishonesty. However, the prior instances must be relevant to character for truthfulness; and no prior instance can be so remote in time as to be irrelevant; the cross-examiner must have a good faith factual basis for the incidents which are inconsistent with truthfulness; and in many courts, the incidents must be put forward in a particular format. In several states, this means asking the witness "have you heard" about the incident, not "do you know."

To illustrate such a cross-examination, we assume that the witness whose direct examination appears at the start of this entry is now cross-examined by the attorney for defendant Cannon Parcel Services.

Cross-Examination

Q. Mr. Jones, you say you know Gary Coddington and his reputation for truthfulness?

A. Yes.

Q. Have you heard that he had trouble with the IRS last year, that he was indicted for income tax evasion?

A. I did hear that he had a beef with the IRS.

Q. Did you also hear that three years ago he and his company were accused by the city of shorting the city on a parts order; that they failed to deliver all of the parts ordered by the city and nonetheless billed the city for the full order?

A. I never heard about that.

Final Argument

In the foregoing case, after the cross-examination illustrated above, a couple of possibilities arise for the defense in summation. One form of closing argument might sound like this:

On cross-examination I asked Mr. Jones, the plaintiff's character witness, whether he had heard that Gary Coddington was charged with income tax evasion. He said "yes." Think about that answer. On the one hand, Mr. Jones testifies that the plaintiff has a good reputation for telling the truth. On the other hand, he admits he has heard about the IRS charge against the plaintiff just last year. Mr. Jones must have a pretty strange standard for deciding whether someone has a good reputation for truthfulness. When a person is charged with tax evasion by the IRS, most reasonable people would say that person has a terrible reputation for truthfulness.

What about the reverse of this situation, where there the character witness has never heard reports of misconduct? In the case of prior misconduct by the supported person, of which incidents the character witness is unaware, an equally potent argument may be made. The jury can be alerted to the fact that the character witness expects the jury to believe that he knows the party's reputation for truth-telling, yet has never heard a report about the plaintiff cheating the city. For an expanded form of this sort of jury argument, see R. Carlson, E. Imwinkelried, E. Kionka and K. Strachan, Evidence: Teaching Materials for an Age of Science and Statutes 325 (5th ed. 2002).

Related Matters

In addition to reputation proof, there is an expansion in the Federal Rules and a growing trend in the states to allow personal testimony as to character. Thus, a witness can testify that on the basis of his personal dealings with another, he concludes that other person is truthful and honest.

Proof in criminal cases of relevant trait of character of defendant or victim, see Rules 404(a), 405, Federal Rules of Evidence. Reputation for truth, veracity, honesty, or other similar traits, see Am. Jur. 49 Proof of Facts 649; 82 ALR 3d 531. See also Fed. R. Ev. 803(21).

In this text, see related entries for *Personal Opinion of Character* and *Character and Reputation: Violence.*

Character and Reputation: Violence and Peacefulness

Elements

Evidence of a pertinent trait of character may be offered under Federal Evidence Rule 404(a)(1) by asking a witness questions which cover these points: 1) the reputation testimony which is sought from the witness must relate to reputation for a trait of character which is at issue in the case; 2) some association between the character witness and the defendant is desirable, but not essential; 3) frequent contact by the character witness with individuals who know the defendant, establishing the defendant's favorable or adverse reputation in his neighborhood or community.

Direct Examination

In the case from which the following testimony appears, the accused is charged with criminal assault. The defendant responds by calling a character witness to assert defendant's nonviolent reputation. What follows is testimony drawn from the case of State v. Jackson, a trial for the crime of Aggravated Assault.

Q. *Defense Attorney:* Mr. Witness, do you know the defendant in this case?

A. Yes.

Q. How long and in what capacity have you known him?

A. We have lived in the same neighborhood on the same street for the past few years.

Q. During that time, did you and Mr. Jackson participate on any neighborhood groups, functions or outings?

A. Yes, we did. We both have served on the neighborhood Homeowners Association, and have been active in setting up neighborhood outings—family softball games, swimming parties and 4th of July parties.

Q. During the time that you have lived in the same neighborhood as Mr. Jackson, and served on the Homeowners Association with him, did you have the opportunity to interact with the other neighbors who knew and associated with Mr. Jackson?

A. Yes, I have. Many of us know each other very well. It is a very friendly community.

Q. And do you and your neighbors ever talk about Mr. Jackson with each other?

A. Yes, we have talked about him before. Many times.

Q. Among these neighbors, does Mr. Jackson have a reputation for peacefulness?

A. He most certainly does.

Q. On the basis of your community knowledge, have you formed an opinion as to the reputation of the defendant for peacefulness in his community?

A. Yes.

Q. What is that opinion?

A. He has a great reputation. He is well-known as being peaceful and even-tempered.

Rule References

Federal Evidence Rule 404(a)(1) and (2) allow admission of a person's trait of character. Rule 405 prescribes the manner of proof. These rules provide as follows:

Rule 404(a)

(1) *Character of Accused.* Evidence of a pertinent trait of character offered by an accused, or by the prosecution to rebut the same, or if evidence of a trait of character of the alleged victim of the crime is offered by an accused and admitted under rule 404(a)(2), evidence of the same trait of character of the accused offered by the prosecution;

(2) *Character of Alleged Victim.* Evidence of a pertinent trait of character offered by an accused, or by the prosecution to rebut the same, or evidence of a character trait of peacefulness of the alleged victim offered by the prosecution in a homicide case to rebut evidence that the alleged victim was the first aggressor.

Federal Evidence Rule 405(a) provides: "In all cases in which evidence of character or a trait of character of a person is admissible, proof may be made by testimony as to reputation or by testimony in the form of an opinion. On cross-examination, inquiry is allowable into relevant specific instances of conduct."

Federal Evidence Rule 803(21) provides a hearsay exception for reputation proof, allowing "[r]eputation of a person's character among associates or in the community."

Cases and Authorities

The choice, in a criminal case, as to whether to initiate character proof to establish the probable conduct of a party belongs to the accused. *United States v. Gilliland*, 586 F.2d 1384 (10th Cir. 1978). Often the defendant will do just that, seeking to portray himself as a stable, responsible family person, the type of person who would be unlikely to commit an unprovoked battery. The trial proof near the start of this section illustrates the point. In an assault case, the defendant's lack of any tendency to violence amounts to a pertinent trait of character. As to other provable character traits in criminal cases, see Annot., 49 A.L.R. Fed 478, 480–81.

After favorable defense testimony, the prosecutor may attack in two ways: 1) cross-examination of the defendant's "good character" witness; 2) the prosecutor calling her own character witness in rebuttal, to reflect adversely on the accused.

The government is entitled to cross-examine a defendant's reputation witness with "have you heard" questions which raise specific instances of the defendant's prior misconduct. However, such a cross is not unrestricted. When the prosecutor cross-examines the sort of witness whose testimony is illustrated in the foregoing Q. and A., it is subject to limitations, including: 1) defendant's prior misconduct which is inquired about must relate directly to the character trait at issue; 2) there must be a sound, good-faith factual basis for the cross-examination question; 3) its form may not be guilt-assuming; it may not ask the witness if his opinion might be changed because the defendant committed the offense for which he is being prosecuted, and is guilty of the current crime. *United States v. Candelaria–Gonzalez*, 547 F.2d 291, 294 (5th Cir. 1977).

Cross-examining a defendant's character witness with specific instances, see *United States v. Green*, 305 F.3d 422, 430–31 (6th Cir. 2002)(there was direct testimony as to defendant's good character and status as a law-abiding citizen, provided by defense character witnesses; government could cross-examine witnesses regarding their knowledge of alleged seizure of $18,000 from defendant, and the trial judge appropriately ended this line of questioning when witnesses denied knowledge of incident; appellate court noted that relevant specific instances of conduct only go to accuracy of character witnesses testimony).

When producing a "good character" witness, the direct examiner frequently asks the witness about the defendant's reputation in the community. Courts have relaxed the definition of "community" for purposes of the reputation rules. See *United States v. Mandel*, 591 F.2d 1347 (4th Cir. 1979)(a particular law office can constitute a community); *United States v. Oliver*, 492 F.2d 943, 945–47 (8th Cir. 1974)(reputation for truth and veracity in college dormitory community); *O'Bryan v. State*, 591 S.W.2d 464, 476 (Tex. Crim. App. 1979)(community includes business circle); *Freeman v. State*, 132 Ga.App. 742, 745, 209 S.E.2d 127, 130–31 (1974)(church congregation).

Prosecutors are not barred from proving favorable traits of a victim of a crime, where relevant. When an assault victim's peaceful traits have been attacked by the defense, the prosecution can shore up the victim with favorable reputation testimony from a friend or neighbor of the victim.

Moreover, the prosecutor can defend the victim of a homicide in this fashion when the defendant claims the victim started the fight, or otherwise came at him. See Federal Evidence Rule 404(a)(2).

Comment

Trait evidence may be either good or bad. The earlier passage in this entry supplies proof of good character. Bad character may also be shown. In an assault case, for example, a prosecutor may resort to evidence of a defendant's violent nature, as demonstrated by community reputation. The defendant must first initiate the issue by attacking the assault victim's reputation or by supplying good character proof during the defense case-in-chief. After the defendant's attempt in a criminal assault case to build up his character for peacefulness, the prosecutor is entitled to rebut by proving the violent character of the accused.

In the following example, the defendant has already attacked the character of the victim of an assault with proof of the victim's assaultive character. The accused also presented a reputation witness during the defense case to swear to the good repute of the accused for peacefulness. Now in rebuttal, the prosecutor calls Waldo Y. Carrier to respond.

Q. Mr. Carrier, do you know the defendant?

A. Yes.

Q. How do you know him?

A. He lives in my neighborhood, near my house.

Q. How long has he lived near you?

A. About three years.

Q. Have you had the opportunity to visit with other neighbors about whether he is a peaceful person?

A. Many times.

Q. Has he developed a reputation for either violence or nonviolence?

A. Yes, he certainly has.

Q. Can you give us your assessment of his community reputation in that regard?

A. Yes. It is bad. The defendant is known as an aggressive, violent man. That is his reputation.

Prosecutor: Thank you, Mr. Carrier. That's all.

The defendant opens himself up to this form of attack when he puts on his own good character proof during the defense case. Additionally, by virtue of a December 1, 2000 amendment to Rule 404, once the defendant attacks the victim's reputation for peacefulness, the defendant is subject to the form of character attack illustrated above.

Rule 404(a) proof, whether positive or negative, is largely restricted to criminal cases. Most courts construe Federal Rules 404–05 as generally precluding the circumstantial use of character evidence in civil cases. *Ginter v. Northwestern Mut. Life Ins. Co.,* 576 F.Supp. 627, 628 (E.D. Ky. 1984). See R. Carlson, E. Imwinkelried, T. Kionka & K. Strachan, Evidence: Teaching Materials for an Age of Science and Statutes 327 (5th ed. 2002).

On the other hand, *character proof regarding a witness' credibility* applies fully in civil or criminal litigation. This is character proof under Federal Evidence Rule 608. For details on the credibility issue, see *Character and Reputation: Truthfulness* in this text. Character may be proved by personal opinion as well as community reputation. For the form of testimony when eliciting a witness' personal opinion of another's character (as opposed to his assessment of community reputation), see the entry in this text for *Personal Opinion of Character.*

Coconspirator Statements

Elements

To prove up a statement made by one conspirator in order to use it against another conspirator, there needs to be evidence on the following elements: 1) prior to the current trial the defendant participated in a criminal agreement; 2) a confederate of the defendant made a declaration in furtherance of the conspiracy while the conspiracy was active and ongoing; 3) a witness who heard the conspirator make the remark testifies to it, and the content of the declaration is relevant to the case.

Direct Examination

Q. **(by prosecutor in a bank robbery case)** Mr. Paul, what is your business?

A. I own a gun shop.

Q. On December 23, did anyone connected with this trial enter your shop?

A. Yes. Wabash Zack Kilgore came in about noon. I had met him once before.

Q. How had you met him?

A. In early December, the defendant over there (indicating the accused Lewis Lefty) came in with the guy and introduced him. I knew the defendant from previous business deals we had done together a couple of times.

Q. Moving again to December 23, the date you mentioned earlier, did you talk with Wabash Kilgore?

A. Yes.

Q. What did he say?

Objection by defense: Hearsay, your honor.

Prosecutor: Co-conspirator declaration, your honor.

Court: Overruled.

Q. **(by prosecutor)** Will you please answer the question?

A. The man said "Lefty and me need a couple of shotguns. The barrels will be a little shorter when we get done working on them." When I asked why they were going to saw the barrels off, he said: "We are going to make a little withdrawal from Customs Bank."

Rule Reference

Federal Rule of Evidence 801(d)(2)(E) provides that a statement is not hearsay if the statement is offered against a party and is a statement by a coconspirator of a party which was made "during the course and in furtherance of the conspiracy."

Cases and Authorities

Defendant's participation in the conspiratorial combine must be established. Satisfying this element, see *United States v. Capelton*, 350 F.3d 231, 241–42 (1st Cir. 2003)(finding predicate requirement that prosecution prove defendant involved in conspiracy in order for admission of co-conspirator statements was satisfied by marked bill from transaction between co-defendants as well as surveillance video depicting transaction). Where the elements are proved, courts are not reluctant to admit declarations of one conspirator as evidence against another. See *United States v. Newton*, 326 F.3d 253, 259–60 (1st Cir. 2003) (upholding trial court finding that statements regarding past murders satisfied requirement that co-conspirator statements furthered conspiracy where conversation served important function of reassuring traffickers that drug organization effectively addressed threats to security and profitability); *United States v. Vega*, 285 F.3d 256, 264–65 (3d Cir. 2002)(district court properly admitted notebooks and cellular phone conversations as coconspirator statements); *United States v. Campbell*, 268 F.3d 1, 5–6 (1st Cir. 2001)(district court properly admitted coconspirator statements).

Comment

When offering conspirator declarations, there is a burden on the government to demonstrate the existence of a conspiracy, defendant's membership in it, and that the declarant conspirator was speaking in an effort to advance the conspiracy. As a rule, there must be corroboration of defendant's participation in the conspiracy in cases where the government relies primarily on the declaration of a coconspirator to show this element.

While most conspiracies will be demonstrated in criminal cases, there is no restriction in the rule to this form of litigation. Where relevant, coconspirator statements may be received in civil cases. See *World of Sleep, Inc. v. La–Z–Boy Chair Co.*, 756 F.2d 1467 (10th Cir. 1985).

Hearsay statements made by one conspirator against another which are made *after* the conspiracy has ended are not admissible. As to duration, a conspiracy is generally deemed to be over when its objective has been carried out, when the last of the conspirators have been arrested, or when the objectives of the conspiracy have been frustrated and cannot be completed.

The coconspirator's declaration can be made in the presence of the defendant or in the defendant's absence. The accused need not be present in order for his cohort's declaration to be admissible against the defendant. In this respect the coconspirator doctrine is much like the agent admissions rule, under which a party's agent is able to bind the principal if the declaration is made during the former's employment. Coconspirator declarations, see *Bourjaily v. United States*, 483 U.S. 171, 107 S.Ct. 2775, 97 L.Ed.2d 144 (1987).

Computer Records

Elements

To prove up records generated or maintained by computer, the following elements should be satisfied: 1) there is a reliable procedure for inputting information into the computer as well as retrieving data from it; 2) the witness or someone under her supervision secured a printout of identified data; 3) proper procedures were used in securing the printout; 4) the witness can identify the printout; 5) the witness is qualified to validate the foregoing steps, usually an employee involved with the handling or supervision of computer work in the business which generated the computer record.

Direct Examination

Q. Mr. Fairchild, as director of business services for Carson Computer Service Bureau, what services does your division perform for Wagner Motors, the defendant in this case?

A. We maintain their sales records, as we do for a number of companies.

Q. I show you a document that was previously marked as defendant's exhibit A for identification and ask you if you can identify it?

A. Yes.

Q. Will you please tell us what the document is?

A. The document is the monthly sales report for Wagner Motor Manufacturing Company for the months from June through September, 1999.

Q. Do you know who prepared exhibit A?

A. Carson Computer Service Bureau.

Q. And the employee?

A. I was in charge of preparing it.

Q. Would you tell us how it was prepared?

A. Exhibit A is a computer printout which contains all of the sales information for the Wagner Motor Manufacturing Company for a four month period. It was generated by the computer utilizing a program which I wrote for the purpose of preparing exhibit A.

Q. Can you tell us what the program does?

A. Yes. On a daily basis Service Bureau dumps all of its disk information onto tape, magnetic tape. These tapes are stored in our tape library. The program which I designed reads the tapes which contain the details of all of the orders received by Wagner during the relevant period. It also selects information regarding any returns of products, and information regarding payments. It then totals all of this information to produce the gross sales in dollar amounts, and the number of returned units, and it computes the total sales by subtracting returns from gross sales.

Q. How did you go about writing this program?

A. I took programming code sheets and wrote the various instructions necessary for locating the required data. The code sheet contents were then entered into the computer and compiled. When the computer compiles a program it takes the instructions written by the programmer and converts them into machine readable code understood by the computer.

Q. Now once the program was compiled, what happened?

A. After creating test data and verifying that the program functioned accurately, I then instructed the computer room to process all Wagner tapes for the months of June, July, August and September, 2004, using the program I had written. The operator took the tapes and my program processed the tapes using my program, and generated exhibit A.

Q. In writing this program for Exhibit A did you employ the normal procedures of the Service Bureau?

A. Yes, I followed normal procedures for writing this program.

Counsel: Your honor, we offer defendant's exhibit A into evidence.

Court: It will be received.

Counsel: With the court's permission, I would like to circulate exhibit A to the jury at this time.

Court: Permission granted.

Rule References

Two rules are often applicable to computer records. The first is the rule allowing business records to be received over a hearsay objection. The second is the rule permitting voluminous data to be summarized. These two rules provide as follows:

Federal Evidence Rule 803(6).

Records of regularly conducted activity. A memorandum, report, record, or data compilation, in any form, of acts, events, conditions, opinions, or diagnoses, made at or near the time by, or from information transmitted by, a person with knowledge, if kept in the course of a regularly conducted business activity, and if it was the regular practice of that business activity to make the memorandum, report, record or data compilation, all as shown by the testimony of the custodian or other qualified witness, or by certification that complies with Rule 902(11), Rule 902(12), or a statute permitting certification, unless the source of information or the method or circumstances of preparation indicated lack of trustworthiness. The term "business" as used in this paragraph includes business, institution, association, profession, occupation, and calling of every kind, whether or not conducted for profit.

Federal Evidence Rule 1006. Summaries.

The contents of voluminous writings, recordings, or photographs which cannot conveniently be examined in court may be presented in the form of a chart, summary, or calculation. The originals, or duplicates, shall be made available for examination or copying, or both, by other parties at reasonable time and place. The court may order that they be produced in court.

Cases and Authorities

Cases include *United States v. Fujii*, 301 F.3d 535, 539 (7th Cir. 2002)(admitting printouts of airline's check-in and reservation records where manager testified that records were made from information transmitted from person with knowledge, made at or near time the information was received, regular business practice was to make entries into computer system, and records were kept as part of regular business activity; the court noted that an INS request that information be printed out does not deprive printout of business-record character); *Sea-Land Service, Inc. v. Lozen Intern., L.L.C.,* 285 F.3d 808, 819–20 (9th Cir. 2002)(for the purpose of Federal Rule of Evidence 803(6), it is immaterial that the business record was maintained in a computer rather than in company books).

One expert has wisely observed: "Even before computer records became commonplace, the courts have held that computer records and reports were just another form of a business record, that can be admitted so long as they meet the requirements of the Business Records Statute." N. Dickert, Georgia Handbook on Foundations and Objections § 5.9 (2003).

Comment

Computer records and data compilations require the litigator to show input procedures which supplied the computer with information. Several courts also require a showing that the electronic equipment is recognized as standard, or established as accurate. Foundation requirements, see *In re Guardianship of Smith*, 109 Ill.App.3d 786, 65 Ill.Dec. 300, 441 N.E.2d 92 (5th Dist. 1982).

To authenticate computer records, a qualified witness may be the one who prepared the record, or another who is familiar with the circumstances of preparation. It is clear that the admissibility of computerized private business records depends upon the establishment of a proper foundation. Admission is usually sought, as has generally been the case, through the business records rule. Under a number of cases, counsel has proceeded under the voluminous writings exception to the best evidence rule, or under state statutes providing for the admission of computerized corporate business records. Proceeding under a voluminous writings/best evidence rule theory, see Annotation, Admissibility of evidence summaries under Uniform Evidence Rule 1006, 59 ALR 4th 971. Expanded proofs for computer records, see 14 Am. Jur. Proof of Facts 2d 173, §§ 26–37.

Other references on proving computer records include 7 ALR 4th 8; 71 ALR 3d 232; 11 ALR 3d 1377, 41 Am. Jur. Trials 445.

On business records as well as summaries, see the entries in this text for *Business Records* and for *Summaries*.

Email and FAX Authentication

One expert has suggested that since an email is an electronic letter, it should be analyzed similarly to other correspondence. In a breach of contract case where the buyer sues for damages, he suggests the following questions:

Q. *Buyer's Attorney:* Mr. Jones (buyer), how did you come to be interested in this product?

A. I saw it advertised on the internet and responded to the person I thought to be the seller.

Q. Do you recall that person's email address?

A. It was seller@aol.com.

Q. After sending the email, did you have an occasion to talk with the seller?

A. Yes, he called after receiving my email. He also said he would send me an email with a time and place to meet to see the hutch.

Q. Did you receive the email from him?

A. Yes.

Q. Was it from the same email address you had responded to the original ad?

A. Yes, it was seller@aol.com.

Q. Did you respond to this email?

A. Yes I did. I hit the reply function to confirm the date and time for the meeting.

Q. Did you meet?

A. Yes we did, at the time agreed to in the emails.

Q. After the meeting, did you make an offer?

A. Yes I did, by email sent to seller@aol.com.

Q. Did you receive a reply to your offer?

A. Yes, he accepted my offer by email.

Q. Mr. Jones, I hand you a document marked plaintiff's exhibit one and ask you to identify it.

A. This is the email I received from the seller at seller@aol.com confirming the contract price and accepting my offer to buy the product.

Q. Your honor, at this time I tender plaintiff's exhibit one.

See N. Dickert, Georgia Handbook on Foundations and Objections § 5.9 (2003), where the foregoing email proof appears. Added details on introducing email evidence, see Note, Anthony D. Dreyer, *When the Postman Beeps Twice: The Admissibility of Electronic Mail Under the Business Records Exception to the Federal Rules of Evidence,* 64 Fordham L. Rev. 2285 (1996). Case authority, see *B.S. ex rel. Schneider v. Board of Sch. Trs.,* 255 F.Supp.2d 891, 893–94 (N.D. Ind. 2003)(stating that affidavit of e-mail recipient was an acceptable method for authenticating e-mail message).

Another technological advance, in addition to computer records and Email, is a document sent by FAX. Some courts have passed approvingly on the authentication of FAXed documents. See *People v. Hagan,* 145 Ill.2d 287, 302–04, 164 Ill.Dec. 578, 583 N.E.2d 494, 500–02 (1991)(finding FAXed document sufficiently authenticated based on FAX machine operator's testimony that document was sent from her store and store's FAX machine was operating properly at time transmitted, and testimony of officer in real estate firm that FAX was delivered to his desk on same day document was transmitted); *United States v. Khorozian,* 333 F.3d 498, 506 (3d Cir. 2003) (noting that ordinarily FAX sender authenticates document by testifying to foundational facts, but finding FAX recipient's testimony sufficient to authenticate FAX where defendant sent FAX and did not take stand because party exercised Fifth Amendment right against self incrimination).

Confessions

Elements

Prosecutors will frequently attempt to prove up admissions and confessions in criminal cases. This is accomplished when the following elements are established: 1) a witness, often a law enforcement officer who secured an admission or confession from a criminal defendant, authenticates the defendant's statement; 2) the statement, whether oral or written, is inconsistent with the defendant's position at trial; 3) constitutional rules have been complied with in securing the evidence.

Direct Examination

Q. (by prosecutor) Detective Wagner, did you immediately begin interrogating the defendant when you met him in the interview room after his arrest?

A. No. I told him that he had a right to remain silent, that anything he said could and would be used against him, and that he had a right to talk to an attorney before any questions were asked. Then I said that if he could not afford to hire an attorney and have one present before and during any questioning, the court would appoint a lawyer for him without charge. Next, I asked him if he understood his rights.

Q. What did he say, if anything?

A. He said he fully understood his rights, but that he still wanted to talk to us.

Q. What did you do next?

A. I asked him to read over a printed waiver form which contains the rights I have just explained, and after reading it he signed it in my presence, indicating his willingness to talk.

(executed form is received in evidence)

Q. What did you do next?

A. I asked him what happened, and he told me.

Q. What did he say?

A. He said he shot his wife.

Rule Reference

Federal Rule of Evidence 801(d)(2)(A) provides that a statement is not hearsay if the statement is offered against a party and is "the party's own statement, in either and individual or a representative capacity."

Cases and Authorities

Miranda v. Arizona, 384 U.S. 436, 86 S.Ct. 1602, 16 L.Ed.2d 694 (1966) establishes the constitutional parameters for a valid confession. See also *United States v. Fernandez*, 172 F.Supp.2d 1265, 1274 (C.D. Cal. 2001)(statement by defendant to witness which indicated defendant's association with Mexican mafia, statement had particularized guarantees of trustworthiness under circumstances where defendant's statement was made to close friend, and thus was reliable and admissible). On the hearsay aspect of this mode of proof, see *United States v. Dukagjini*, 326 F.3d 45, 62–63 (2d Cir. 2003)(holding witness's testimony that defendant told him about defendant's possession of gun as non-hearsay admission by party-opponent and admitting testimony as party's own statement).

Comment

Introduction of a criminal defendant's statements requires compliance with hearsay norms as well as constitutional requirements. The hearsay bar is avoided by reliance upon the admissions doctrine. Constitutional requirements must also be satisfied. Constitutional challenges may take two forms, one that the confession is involuntary and the other that *Miranda* was violated. Compliance with *Miranda* is demonstrated in the foregoing proof. While a written waiver is not mandatory, it does strengthen the prosecutor's hand when a confession is challenged.

It is to be remembered that a showing of compliance with *Miranda* standards is needed in custodial interrogation situations, but is not invariably required when a defendant's threshold declarations are offered.

When voluntariness is challenged, the rules may be satisfied by showing that the confession was not the product of intimidation, threats or force. In many jurisdictions, the defendant's confession must be corroborated by independent evidence of the defendant's complicity in the crime. Admissions and confessions, see *Admissions,* supra. Corroboration of confession, see 1 Am. Jur. Proof of Facts 161, Proof No. 8 (Supp.).

Custody of Exhibits

Elements

When introducing physical evidence, the following testimony should be elicited from an authenticating witness: 1) the witness testifies about how she seized, discovered or otherwise received a physical object; 2) the nature of the physical object is described; 3) upon taking possession of the object, the witness observed its appearance, perhaps marked it, and thereafter safeguarded it; 4) upon seeing the object in court at trial, the witness affirms that the exhibit is the one she initially secured; 5) this item of real evidence is in the same condition as when she initially discovered or received the object.

Direct Examination

Q. *by Prosecutor:* Officer Jones, at the site of the break-in to which you were called, did you find anything?

A. Yes, a cardboard carton which appeared to have been ripped open.

Q. What, if anything, did you do with this carton?

A. I examined it for fingerprints. Since none were visible, I used the appropriate forensic tests and developed latent prints. They were photographed, then I marked this carton for identification.

Q. What kind of marks did you make?

A. I affixed a label to the carton and marked the date, case number, place where found, and my initials.

Q. What, if anything, did you do with this carton?

A. I took it to the station and placed it in the safe where it has been since I brought it to court today.

Q. I now show you a cardboard carton, prosecution exhibit C for identification, and ask you if you recognize it?

A. Yes.

Q. Is this the carton about which you just gave testimony?

A. Yes.

Q. How can you identify it?

A. From the identification label here **(indicating)** which I placed on it.

Q. Does it appear to be tampered with or altered in any way?

A. No. It is in the same condition as when I found it.

(Offer and reception into evidence occurs next).

Rule Reference

Federal Evidence Rule 901(a) provides as follows: *General provision.* The requirement of authentication or identification as a condition precedent to admissibility is satisfied by evidence sufficient to support a finding that the matter in question is what its proponent claims.

Cases and Authorities

See *United States v. Carlos* Cruz, 352 F.3d 499, 506 (1st Cir. 2003)(concluding machine guns properly authenticated where agent testified that weapons were seized immediately after arrest, taken to police headquarters, and thereafter remained in custody of Bureau of Alcohol, Tobacco, and Firearms agent); *United States v. Jackson,* 345 F.3d 59, 65 (2d Cir. 2003)(finding government established sufficient chain of custody with videotape showing defendant giving a substance to informant, agent's testimony of government's surveillance of informant before, during, and after transaction, agent's testimony regarding field testing and storage of drugs, and testimony of chemist who tested substance). Chain of custody rules are often enforced more vigorously in criminal than in civil cases. See, e.g., *Cooper v. Eagle River Memorial Hosp., Inc.*, 270 F.3d 456, 463–64 (7th Cir. 2001)(court admitted numbered pathology slide even though hospital failed to establish uninterrupted chain of custody).

Comment

Real evidence consists of an object which played a role in the events described at trial. This might be the gun in a homicide case. The item will be marked as an exhibit, and chain of custody considerations emerge. Since the purpose of the chain of custody rule is to prevent tampering, loss or mistake with respect to an exhibit, authenticating testimony is required to negative these possibilities. When real or original physical evidence which has an historical connection to the facts of the case is offered, testimony should be elicited that it was appropriately secured and retained until its presentation upon trial. Items of real evidence that are readily identifiable are often treated with more liberal authentication rules. Chain of custody is frequently critical with items that are not readily identifiable. The dichotomy between hard evidence and items not readily identifiable was discussed in *State v. Houston*, 439 N.W.2d 173, 179 (Iowa 1989):

> We have consistently held that where the exhibits consist of solid objects which are not easily susceptible to undetected alteration, the exhibits may be admitted into evidence despite a break in the chain of custody. *State v. Limerick*, 169 N.W.2d 538, 541 (Iowa 1969). "Where the possibility of alteration of an exhibit is slight, the materiality of the alteration remote, and the exhibit has otherwise been properly identified we have dispensed with a showing of continuous custody." Id. (concerning admission of a gun).

Chain of custody rules were reviewed when scissors were received in evidence in *Westwood v. State*, 693 P.2d 763 (Wyo. 1985). The scissors were authenticated as the weapon in this aggravated assault case, and the court ruled their admission to be proper:

> [An] article may be received if it is satisfactorily identified, and is shown to the satisfaction of the court that there is no substantial change in the article which would render the evidence misleading. In our judgment these requirements were satisfied with respect to the school scissors.

Id. at 765.

Modest change in an object between time of seizure and trial, see discussion in *Bruce v. State*, 268 Ind. 180, 375 N.E.2d 1042, 1 A.L.R. 4th 616, (1978).

Additional references, see 36 Am. Jur. Proof of Facts 2d 285 **(fingerprints)**; 5 Am. Jur. Proof of Facts 113, at 121 **(evidence receipts, bullets and firearms)**; 29 Am. Jur. Proof of Facts 65 **(firearms)**.

Death [Presumption from Absence]

Elements

To prove the fact of death, a party will rely on these principles: 1) the presumption of death arising from continuous absence requires absence from the decedent's place of residence or usual place of abode, and mere absence from the residence of relatives is often not sufficient; 2) the absence must endure long enough to fulfill the common-law or statutory time requirement, usually seven years but subject to variation in different states; 3) the missing individual must have volition, and must not be a child of tender years; 4) the absence of the individual must be unexplained.

Direct Examination

Q. Ms. Jones, can you tell us the date on which your husband left your home to shop for a new car?

A. I don't recall the exact date, but it was in January of 1998. My birthday is January 23, and a few days later my husband decided to buy a new car.

Q. Did your husband return home later that day?

A. No.

Q. Did he ever return home at any time after his departure for the car dealership?

A. No.

Q. Have you seen your husband at any time during the years that have gone by since he left in January 1998?

Objection by opponent: Irrelevant.

Response by Proponent: Your honor, I intend to show the fact of death through the husband's continuous absence for at least seven years.

Court: Overruled.

Q. Have you seen him since he left?

A. No. The last time I saw him was when he left for the Chrysler dealership with his car keys in his hand.

Rule Reference

Federal Rule of Evidence 301 pertaining to presumptions in general in civil actions and proceedings, provides that in all civil actions and proceedings not otherwise provided for by Act of Congress or by the rules, a presumption imposes on the party against whom it is directed the burden of going forward with evidence to rebut or meet the presumption, but does not shift to such party the burden of proof in the sense of the risk of nonpersuasion, which remains throughout the trial upon the party on whom it was originally cast.

Cases and Authorities

See *In re Estate of Slack*, 195 F.Supp.2d 1052 (N.D. Ill. 2002)(presumption of death is raised where person is continuously absent for seven years from home without explanation, those with whom he would likely communicate have not heard from him or about him, and a diligent search has not resulted in information that he is alive); *Fuller v. American Fed'n of Labor*, 328 F.3d 672, 674 (D.C. Cir. 2003)(stating District of Columbia law regarding presumption of death: "[i]f a person leaves his domicile without a known intention of changing it, and does not return or is not heard from for seven years from the time of his so leaving, he shall be presumed to be dead in any case where his death is in question, unless proof is made that he was alive within that time", citing D.C. Code Ann.

§ 14–701 (2001), and noting that presumption of death extends only to fact of death, leaving precise date of death a question of fact to be resolved).

Comment

Proof that a person has disappeared from his home and has absented himself for at least seven years and that during this time those who would be expected to hear from him have received no tidings and after diligent inquiry have been unable to find his whereabouts, raises a presumption that he died at some time during the seven year period. McCormick, Evidence § 343 (5th ed. 1999). See *Penrose v. Heckler*, 566 F.Supp. 301 (D.Nev. 1983). While there is some authority to the contrary, the majority of cases require search and inquiry to ascertain the whereabouts of the absentee. Expanding upon the trial proof above, eliciting testimony from an appropriate witness that the children of the family have heard nothing from their father strengthens the proponent's position. This comes under the heading of lack of word from the decedent to likely recipients.

Of course, the fact of death can also be established by different means where direct or supportive evidence is available. This includes proof by an official certificate of death, church records, entries in a family Bible, or by direct proof. A witness' testimony that he saw the decedent's body falls into the latter category and is deemed competent. These forms of proof are discussed in 28 Am. Jur. Proof of Facts 2d 81.

Other forms of proof of death, see *Age* and *Public Records* in this text.

Declarations Against Interest

Elements

Sometimes an out of court statement seems, on the surface at least, to be adverse to the person who uttered it. A speaker talks against his own interests. Such a hearsay declaration is admissible when: 1) an out-of-court speaker makes a relevant statement which is against himself; 2) it is readily apparent that the content of the statement was contrary to the interest of the speaker; 3) the speaker was talking against his own pecuniary or proprietary interest, or the speaker's words potentially exposed the declarant to civil or criminal liability; 4) the speaker is unavailable at trial, but a witness who heard him speak attends the trial and is ready to testify.

Direct Examination

Q. Ms. Boswell, you realize this is a civil case and my client, the defendant, has been sued for driving recklessly?

A. Yes.

Q. Are you aware of the seriousness of the accident?

A. Yes, I know one person was killed.

Q. Where were you on the afternoon of February 19, 2004?

A. Corner of Bush and Elm Streets, where the wreck happened.

Q. Did you see anything unusual there?

A. Yes, as I walked up to the corner I saw the two cars badly smashed. One of the drivers and some of the onlookers were milling about. Police had just arrived.

Q. Did anyone say anything to you?

A. Yes, a Mr. Tafoya whom I knew said something important to me.

Q. What did he say?

Objection by Plaintiff's Attorney: Hearsay, your honor.

Defense: I will lay the foundation for a declaration against interest, your honor.

Court: Proceed.

Q. Ms. Boswell, you said you knew the speaker. Did Mr. Tafoya confide to you any information which was detrimental or harmful to himself?

A. He certainly did.

Q. What did he say?

A. He was speaking in a low voice. Tafoya said "I tell you Boswell, the police think that my pal Popeye Slavens over there was driving the car. But really it was me."

Q. Where was Popeye?

A. Laying on the ground unconscious. Apparently he had been riding with my friend Tafoya, as a passenger.

Q. Paul "Popeye" Slavens is my client in this suit. He is being sued for bad driving. But you heard the other man at the scene say *he* was driving the car, *not* Popeye.

A. That's exactly what Tafoya said.

Rule Reference

Rule 804(b)(3), as it is slated to be revised on or after December 1, 2004, controls this hearsay exception. After requiring that the declarant be unavailable, the rule stipulates the conditions for admissibility.

Federal Rule of Evidence 804(b)(3). Statement against interest. A statement that was at the time of its making so far contrary to the declarant's pecuniary or proprietary interest, or so far tended to subject the declarant to civil or criminal liability, or to render invalid a claim by the declarant against another, that a reasonable person in the declarant's position would not have made the statement unless believing it to be true. But a statement tending to expose the declarant to criminal liability is admissible under this subdivision in the following circumstances only: (A) if offered in a civil case or to exculpate an accused in a criminal case, it is supported by corroborating circumstances that clearly indicate its trustworthiness, or (B) if offered to inculpate an accused, it is supported by particularized guarantees of trustworthiness. (Author's note: This is Rule 804(b)(3) as it is scheduled to be revised by the proposed 2004 amendment of the rule; while the language of the present rule is identical to most of this new revision, the new rule incorporates a couple of fresh provisions).

Cases and Authorities

In *United States v. Katsougrakis*, 715 F.2d 769 (2d Cir. 1983) the defendants owned a business which was losing money. They hired an arsonist to burn down their building. The unexpected occurred, and the arsonist was severely burned in his own fire. Before he died, he talked to a friend. The friend asked if "you [the arsonist] got paid to burn this place up?" The arsonist, who was in the hospital wrapped from head to toe in bandages, nodded "yes." Shortly thereafter, he died. At trial of the business owners, the arsonist's friend appeared as a prosecution witness. The parties conceded that a "nod" is a statement for purposes of the hearsay rule. However, since the "nod" clearly subjected the arsonist to criminal liability—by affirmatively nodding he admitted complicity in the criminal undertaking—the description of it fell within the hearsay exception. Moreover, this declaration against penal interest was amply corroborated. A limitation imposed in some subsequent District Court opinions suggested that statements like this must be shown to be especially reliable or particularly trustworthy.

There is an issue regarding such declarations when they are "mixed," that is, where the speaker admits he did something wrong but also seeks to defend or justify himself. Sometimes out-of-court statements by unavailable declarants are partly self-serving and partly against the declarant's interest. In such situations, only the "against interest" portion is admissible, unless the two statements are so inextricably interwoven as to be inseparable. *Williamson v. United States*, 512 U.S. 594, 600, 114 S.Ct. 2431, 129 L.Ed.2d 476 (1994)(Rule 804(b)(3) (this hearsay exception does not allow admission of non-self-inculpatory statements)).

Comment

A statement which exposes a declarant to criminal liability which is offered to exonerate the accused or, in a civil case, to exculpate one of the parties must be corroborated. Rule 804(b)(3) will be amended effective on or after December 1, 2004 to add the civil case proviso to the corroboration requirement. The proposed new rule provides that the corroborating circumstances requirement applies to all declarations against penal interest, whether proffered in civil or criminal cases.

Clause (B) of the rule confirms the requirement that the prosecution must provide a showing of "particularized guarantees of trustworthiness" when a declaration against penal interest is offered against an accused in a criminal case. See *Lilly v. Virginia*, 527 U.S. 116, 134–38, 119 S.Ct. 1887, 144 L.Ed.2d 117 (1999).

Finally, a 2004 decision of the United States Supreme Court mandates that many declarations against interest must be cross-examined. The confrontation clause applies to out-of-court statements which are testimonial—that is, statements a declarant would expect to be used to prosecute a person. Accomplice confessions to police fall into this category, and require cross-examination of the declarant. *Crawford v. Washington,* ___ U.S. ___, 124 S.Ct. 1354, 158 L.Ed.2d 177 (2004).

For more on establishing unavailability of a hearsay declarant, see provisions defining Unavailability of Declarant in Rule 804(a).

Dying Declarations

Elements

When a declarant, now deceased, previously spoke about a relevant event, the lawyer who seeks to prove up the statement needs to consider the dying declarations doctrine. The elements include: 1) the declarant had a sense of impending death, established by words or actions of the declarant or by circumstantial evidence; 2) he or she spoke under the influence of this sense of impending death; 3) the declarant is dead or otherwise unavailable; 4) the statement relates to the facts and circumstances of what the declarant believes to be his impending death; 5) the trial witness heard the communication from the declarant.

Direct Examination

Q. (by plaintiff's attorney) Doctor, why did you go to the emergency room at St. Francis hospital?

A. It was a serious accident. That is why I was summoned. The death certificate shows that a passenger in one of the cars—as it turns out, in the plaintiff's Buick—lapsed into a coma and died as the result of cerebral hemorrhage.

Q. Doctor, were you with the passenger at the time he became conscious?

A. Yes. I was able to speak to this gentleman in the emergency room before he lapsed into a coma.

Q. So you did talk to my client's passenger at the hospital?

A. Yes.

Q. What did he say?

Objection: Calls for hearsay, your honor.

Plaintiff's Attorney: A dying declaration will be established, your honor.

Court: Overruled.

Q. Please tell us what the passenger said?

A. He looked to me like he was on his last legs and as I recall it, the passenger said, "I know I'm done for. That other driver ran us down like we weren't even there when he ran the red light."

Rule Reference

Federal Evidence Rule 804(b). Hearsay exceptions. The following are not excluded by the hearsay rule if the declarant is unavailable as a witness:

. . . .

(2) *Statement under belief of impending death.* In a prosecution for homicide or in a civil action or proceeding, a statement made by a declarant while believing that the declarant's death was imminent, concerning the cause or circumstances of what the declarant believed to be impending death.

Cases and Authorities

The traditional common law view is that dying declarations are limited to homicide cases where the speaker died. The Federal Rules of Evidence expanded the concept to permit introduction in civil cases and in cases where the speaker does not die. Thus, even in cases where the victim of an attack survives, if he speaks under a belief in his impending death, the declaration is admitted. The requirement of a sense of impending death has been vigorously enforced by the courts. See *Sternhagen v. Dow Co.*, 108 F.Supp.2d 1113, 1118 (D. Mont. 1999)(declarant did not believe his death was "imminent" for purposes of the dying declaration exception to the hearsay rule where he expected to live another 3–6 months).

So has the requirement that the declarant speak or write about the circumstances causing his death. See *United States v. Angleton*, 269 F.Supp.2d 878, 887–88, 891 (S.D. Tex. 2003) (granting government motion in limine to exclude notes found in jail cell of suicide victim where comments and lengthy postscripts suggest documents were written over period of time, and statements about past events were not about cause and circumstances of death and did not explain predicament that brought declarant to death's door).

Comment

Civil cases and homicide prosecutions are the sorts of litigation wherein the proponent may successfully introduce dying declarations under Federal Evidence Rule 804(b)(2), but not in felonies at large. Many states have adopted new rules of evidence in the federal pattern. In doing so, some have expanded the exception to apply to all criminal cases, not just homicides, as well as civil litigation. The common law doctrine limited the exception to observed facts, not opinions, and to introduction in criminal homicide cases only. As this passage suggests, these concepts have been expanded by modern law.

Dying declarations today may be cast in the form of opinion. For example, the speaker might say: "The shooter walked right up to me and shot me and I am pretty sure the shooter was Scott."

The declarant's consciousness of impending death may be demonstrated by his own words or may be established by circumstantial evidence.

Easement by Prescription

Elements

Sometimes a party makes a claim to property on account of his unimpeded use of it for a substantial period. To win a prescriptive easement case, these are the elements: 1) the claimant must show that the use was actual, adverse, open, notorious, and continuous; 2) the adverse use by the claimant must have been uninterrupted for the prescribed statutory period. Some courts add the requirement that the use be with the knowledge and acquiescence of the owner of the property on which the easement is located.

Direct Examination

In the following proof, the plaintiff seeks a declaration of easement over a roadway which runs across a neighbor's land.

Q. Mr. Jones, when did you buy the Oak Lake property?

A. 1993.

Q. Will you please describe it?

A. Yes. The lake frontage is 200 feet, and our house faces the lake. Then the lot runs back toward the county road about 100 feet, but not all the way up to the county road.

Q. How do you get from the county road down to the lake?

A. Over a road that cuts across my neighbor's property. My father and I have used that road on a day-to-day basis from the time we bought the Oak Lake property.

Q. Did you receive any indications that your neighbor knew of your use?

Objection by opponent: Irrelevant.

Response by proponent of witness: Your honor, I intend to establish the elements of a prescriptive easement by showing that the plaintiff's use of the road was obvious and well known to the defendant.

Court: Objection overruled.

Q. You may answer my question. Did he indicate to you in any way that he knew of your use?

A. Plenty. His farm house is located just off the road, and several times he waved to me from his window when he was inside as I was driving across the cutover road. Again, he would look over toward me occasionally if he was out in the field when I drove down to the lake. Now he tries to throw logs across it so I can't use it, after all these years.

Rule References

States prescribe the statutory period which must be satisfied in order for a successful claimant to prevail on an easement claim. Some illustrative time provisions include Cal. Civ. § 1007, Cal. Civ. Proc. § 318 (2004)(occupancy for five years confers title by prescription); Conn. Gen. Stat. § 47–37 (2004)(requiring continued uninterrupted use for fifteen years); Ga. Code Ann. § 44–9–54 (2004)(requiring uninterrupted use for seven years for private way); Iowa Code § 564.1 (1992)(requiring adverse possession for ten years); Mass. Gen. Laws ch. 187, § 2 (2003) (requiring continued uninterrupted use for twenty years).

Cases and Authorities

Easement claims continue to appear in court. See *Pascoag Reservoir & Dam, L.L.C. v. Rhode Island*, 217 F.Supp.2d 206, 211–12 (D.R.I. 2002)(stating elements of adverse possession and prescriptive easements under Rhode Island law as open, notorious, hostile, continuous, exclusive possession under claim of right; noting easement by prescription creates right to use and title to use that cannot be revoked); *Tennessee Gas Pipeline Co. v. Mississippi Central R. Co.*, 164 F.Supp.2d 823, 826 (N.D. Miss. 2001)(prescriptive easement of railroad company). See James Smith, Edward Larson, John Kidwell & John Nagle, Property: Cases and Materials 654–58 (2004).

Comment

Prescriptive easements are often established when a landowner repeatedly uses a neighbor's road or alley for access. See *Plettner v. Sullivan*, 214 Neb. 636, 335 N.W.2d 534 (1983) (finding prescriptive easement when claimant and record owner jointly used private road for over 16 years; open use of neighbor's land is presumed to be adverse). See also *Healy v. Roberts*, 109 Ill.App.3d 577, 64 Ill.Dec. 927, 440 N.E.2d 647 (1st Dist. 1982)(easements by prescription over roads and alleys).

Additional cases, see *Hermes v. Fischer*, 226 Ill.App.3d 820, 168 Ill.Dec. 605, 589 N.E.2d 1005 (1992)(claimant continuously cultivated parcel of land for over 20 years; claimant thus proved ownership by adverse possession); *Johnson v. Kaster*, 637 N.W.2d 174 (Iowa 2001)(while there may be distinctions, an easement by prescription is based on the principle of estoppel and is similar to the concept of adverse possession); *Novotny v. Robbins*, 492 N.W.2d 216 (Iowa App. 1992)(title by virtue of acquiescence for period of ten years). Establishment of public prescriptive easement, see 2 Am. Jur. Proof of Facts 3d 197; establishment of private easement, see 2 Am. Jur. Proof of Facts 3d 125.

Excited Utterance

Elements

This important exception to the hearsay rule is established by the following elements: 1) there was a startling event; 2) the person who witnessed the event was traumatized or excited by the occurrence; 3) the excited person spoke in the presence of a witness during the time that the declarant was under the influence of excitement caused by the dramatic event; 4) the witness reports the declarant's words at a trial, hearing or other proceeding.

Direct Examination

Q. **(by defense attorney)** Mr. Pack, did you see the accident?

A. No.

Q. Why did you go the corner?

A. I heard this big crash, it sounded like a cannon. I was standing on my front porch, about 4 houses from the corner. After the noise, I hurried up to the corner of Green and Madison, the place where I heard the noise come from.

Q. What did you see when you got there?

A. Two cars, steam coming from the radiators, they were almost welded together head-on.

Q. Were there any people there?

A. Mr. Wexler. He's an elderly man who lives on our street.

He rushed over to me when he saw me coming toward the intersection.

Q. Did you notice anything unusual about Mr. Wexler?

A. Yes. His hands were shaking and his voice was staccato, very broken. It was also high-pitched.

Q. Without telling us what he said, can·you tell us whether he was talking rapidly or slowly?

A. His speech was unusually fast. I have known him for a long time and have conversed with him on many occasions. This time, he was rushing to tell me the story.

Q. Did you notice anything else about him?

A. He was perspiring heavily. I could see it on his forehead, and when I took his hands to calm him down, his palms were damp.

Q. Was he excited?

A. He was very excited.

Q. What did he say?

A. He told me that the green car, the Dodge, came over the curb and almost knocked him down, then careened back into the street and smacked into the red car.

Rule Reference

Under *Federal Evidence Rule 803(2)*, a statement is not excluded by the hearsay rule when it relates to a startling event or condition and was made "while the declarant was under the stress of excitement caused by the event or condition."

Cases and Authorities

See United States v. Alexander, 331 F.3d 116, 122–24 (D.C. Cir. 2003)(affirming determination that 911 call made fifteen to twenty minutes after threat was admissible as excited utterance where nature of the threats, short lapse of time between threats and 911 call, and fact that recipient called her mother first, all lend support to district court's ruling; noting that although lapse of time between startling event and declarant's statement is relevant to whether statement made under stress of excitement, temporal gap not dispositive and other relevant factors include: characteristics of event, subject matter of statement, whether statement made in response to inquiry, and declarant's age, motive to lie and physical and mental condition); *Woodward v. Williams*, 263 F.3d 1135, 1141 (10th Cir. 2001)(court admitted excited utterance relating to the startling event); *United States v. Brown*, 254 F.3d 454, 458–59 (3d Cir. 2001)(court admitted declarant's statements to law enforcement minutes after observing a man wielding a firearm).

Comment

The numerous hearsay exceptions collected in Federal Evidence Rule 803 are cast in terms of nonapplication of the hearsay bar, rather than making them automatically admissible. Thus, a valid hearsay statement may still be objected to on grounds like irrelevant or prejudicial, even though the proof passes the hearsay test. However, the evidence in the foregoing trial proof is both relevant as well as "good hearsay." It qualifies under Rule 803's excited utterance exception.

Excited utterance, *see United States v. Golden*, 671 F.2d 369, 371 (10th Cir. 1982)(victim's statement to his grandmother occurred within fifteen minutes of startling event, immediately after a high speed flight from the scene of the assault).

Experiments

Elements

When introducing the results of an out-of-court experiment, these are the elements: 1) evidence of an extrajudicial experiment may be admitted if the experiment was conducted under circumstances that were similar to those existing at the time of the litigated occurrence; 2) the person who performed the experiment is competent to do so, and the testing apparatus was suitable for the purpose.

Direct Examination

Q. **(by plaintiff's attorney to chemist in flammable fabric case)** I now show you plaintiff's exhibit A and ask if you recognize it?

A. Yes, I do. It is a nightgown I tested.

Q. How do you recognize it?

A. It was brought to me at my laboratory by your investigator.

Q. For what purpose?

A. To determine the degree of flammability and ascertain whether that flammability reached a hazardous level.

Q. How did you conduct the test?

A. I purchased a nightgown from the same maker that was made out of the same kind of fabric, identical to plaintiff's cotton flannelette nightgown. I placed it on a mannequin of approximately the same height as plaintiff. Using the electric stove in the plaintiff's home, I heated the burner at the same setting as she had done, for the same amount of time. I held the mannequin so the nightgown came into contact with the glowing burner.

Q. What happened?

A. The nightgown ignited immediately.

Rule Reference

Federal Evidence Rule 401. Definition of "Relevant Evidence." "Relevant evidence" means evidence having any tendency to make the existence of any fact that is of consequence to the determination of the action more probable or less probable than it would be without the evidence.

Cases and Authorities

Unless the experiment duplicates in substantially similar manner the original facts and circumstances, it will be held to be irrelevant and will be excluded. See Note, *Experimental Evidence—Similarity of Conditions*, 21 Def. L.J. 512 (1972). In *Jackson v. Fletcher*, 647 F.2d 1020, 1026–28 (10th Cir. 1981), the defendant's accident reconstruction expert testified about a test of a tractor's stopping distance. The court held that the admission of the testimony was error. The court found "vast" differences between the circumstances at the time of the test and those at the time of the collision. The court reversed on classical legal irrelevance grounds; the court stressed that the differences "cause concern that the jury could have been misled." Id.

On the other hand, experimental evidence may be admitted if conditions are similar, even if test conditions do not perfectly correspond to the conditions at issue in the litigation. *Stecyk v. Bell Helicopter Textron, Inc.,* 295 F.3d 408, 412–13 (3d Cir. 2002)(wrongful death action resulting from crash of Osprey aircraft; videotape of manufacturer's tests was not abuse of discretion). Other cases on out-of-court experiments, see *Jodoin v. Toyota Motor Corp.*, 284 F.3d 272 (1st Cir. 2002)(expert tested vehicle of same make and model year as plaintiff's truck, for rollover propensity; district court's standard of "virtually identical" was too narrow, and plaintiff cleared "substantial similarity" hurdle); *Chavez v. Illinois State Police*, 251 F.3d 612, 637 (7th Cir. 2001)(court admitted experiment as evidence that state police had a policy of making stops based on race); *Worthington v. Wal–Mart Stores, Inc.*, 257 F.Supp.2d 1339, 1342 (D. Kan. 2003) (concluding testimony of defendant's textile expert admissible in product liability suit regarding injuries sustained when plaintiff's flannel shirt caught fire while he was welding; defense expert well-qualified to testify in fabric flammability issues, manikin experiments are type reasonably relied upon by experts in the field, and results of expert's testing helpful to jury).

Comment

Tests and experiments of various kinds regularly mark proof in modern trials. See 6 Am. Jur. Proof of Facts 3d 93 § 54 (field test with identical ATV as one involved in accident); 6 Am. Jur. Proof of Facts 3d 195 § 29 (flammable fabric). In-court experiments, see R. Carlson, *Successful Techniques for Civil Trials* 2d § 3:15 (1992).

Fees

Elements

To impact credibility of an opponent's expert, proving his fees for testifying is an important determinant. These can be established in this manner: 1) when cross-examining the expert, ask her what fees she will charge or has charged for providing testimony; 2) also inquire about fees earned for any pretrial reports, tests or workups in the case; 3) where requisite candor is not forthcoming regarding fees, counsel may have to resort to extrinsic proof of the expert's fees.

Cross-Examination

Q. **(by plaintiff's attorney)** Doctor, what is your fee for your time here today?

A. $7,000.

Q. How many times have you testified at the request of Ms. Wallace, the defense attorney in this case?

A. Twice.

Q. And your fee in those two cases?

A. $6,000 in each case.

Rule Reference

Federal Evidence Rule 611(b) provides that credibility may be attacked. The rule provides:

Rule 611(b)

Scope of cross-examination. Cross-examination should be limited to the subject matter of the direct examination and matters affecting the credibility of the witness. The court may, in the exercise of discretion, permit inquiry into additional matters as if on direct examination.

Cases and Authorities

The compensation earned by an expert is deemed to be a "matter affecting the credibility of a witness," and is a proper subject for cross-examination. See *Crowe v. Bolduc*, 334 F.3d 124, 131–32 (1st Cir. 2003)(noting financial incentive of witness is classic bias evidence routinely permitted on cross-examination and although majority rule prohibits hiring of witness on contingent fee basis, where witness under contingent fee agreement is permitted to testify, examination about fee is vital); *United States v. Edwardo–Franco*, 885 F.2d 1002, 1009–10 (2d Cir. 1989)(cross-examination of government's handwriting expert as to whether expert received several thousand dollars each time he testified for government was relevant to show potential bias).

Patient's estate was entitled to cross-examine an expert witness who testified on behalf of an emergency room physician in a medical malpractice action, to show that he had previously testified as an expert witness on behalf of the same physician and that he had been compensated. The amount of money that the physician who was on trial paid the witness in a prior case was a relevant area of inquiry, as it may indicate bias. The probative value of potential bias outweighed any prejudice to the physician on trial resulting from the jury's knowledge that she had been a defendant in an unrelated lawsuit. *Sawyer v. Comerci*, 264 Va. 68, 563 S.E.2d 748 (2002).

Comment

Compensation earned by an expert witness in the current case can be explored on direct examination or exposed by the cross-examiner. Examination of an expert about fees earned in prior cases is not improper under some decisions, but there is a split of authority on the point. The cross-examiner may show that the expert has an interest in the case because of employment for a fee. Apparent bias may be inferred on the part of an expert who is a "professional witness" receiving a substantial part of his income from customary employment on one side of the docket in cases similar to the one on trial. See *Collins v. Wayne Corp.*, 621 F.2d 777, 783–84 (5th Cir. 1980)(holding that cross-examination of an expert witness about payments that he had received for testifying in prior lawsuits was not error). The *Collins* court adds that "[c]ases from the state courts are split" and cites decisions. Financial interest of expert, see 21 Am. Jur. Proof of Facts 2d 73.

Habit or Custom

Elements

To prove a habit for courtroom purposes, the following elements should be established: 1) the actor's response to a particular kind of situation is regular, routine and repeated; 2) the habit is probative of conduct which is relevant to the case.

Direct Examination

Particularly where a person has been killed and cannot testify for herself, habit proof can be vital. In the following case, a pedestrian was struck by a vehicle and died. Her estate's wrongful death suit turns on whether she was within or outside the crosswalk. Although a neighbor did not see the accident, he has seen the deceased cross the street where the death occurred. He is called by the plaintiff.

Q. As a neighbor of Ms. Walker, have you had occasion to see the route that she regularly took to the grocery store?

A. Yes. My house is on the corner, and I have seen her cross that intersection going north on many, many occasions.

Q. How did she cross Oak Street at the point?

A. Ms. Walker always crossed the street in a straight line and directly within the crosswalk.

Rule Reference

Federal Evidence Rule 406. Habit; Routine Practice. Evidence of the habit of a person or of the routine practice of an organization, whether corroborated or not and regardless of the presence of eyewitnesses, is relevant to prove that the conduct of the person or organization on a particular occasion was in conformity with the habit or routine practice.

Cases and Authorities

See *Beard v. Flying J. Inc.*, 116 F.Supp.2d 1077, 1097 (S.D. Iowa 2000), rev'd in part on other grounds, 266 F.3d 792 (8th Cir. 2001)(pattern of co-employee sexual harassment was admissible as habit or pattern evidence under Federal Rule of Evidence 406). The actions of the person must be repeated and specific, not general. See *United States v. Wright*, 206 F.Supp.2d 609, 615–16 (D. Del. 2002)(holding legislator's general tendency to loan money to friends was a general description of his disposition, not a reflexive or automatic habit, and may not be relied upon to prove conformity therewith on this specific occasion).

Because of the danger of abuse in such evidence, habit is never to be lightly established. *Kimberlin v. PM Transport, Inc.*, 264 Va. 261, 563 S.E.2d 665 (2002)(in order for evidence of a person's habit to be admissible to prove that person's conduct on a particular occasion, examples of habit must be numerous and regular).

Comments

The habit of Ms. Walker in the foregoing Q. and A. scenario is highly relevant to whether she was outside the crosswalk when the accident occurred, as claimed by the opposing party. To establish habit, the conduct or practice must be frequent, and under some cases it must be invariable, or, at least consistent.

Business routines and customs are closely related to habit proof. Courts are receptive to proof of regular business practices. The courts tend to admit evidence of business customs more liberally than testimony about personal habits. R. Carlson, E. Imwinkelried, E. Kionka & K. Strachan, Evidence: Teaching Materials for an Age of Science and Statutes 335 (5th ed. 2002): "This may be because there is no confusion between character traits and business practices, as there is between character and [personal] habit, or it may reflect the belief that the need for regularity in business and the organizational sanctions which may exist when employees deviate from the established procedures give extra guarantees that the questioned activity followed the usual custom." 1 McCORMICK, EVIDENCE § 1 195, at 689 (5th ed. 1999).

Proof of routine business practices such as mailing a letter, see 35 Am. Jur. Proof of Facts 2d 589. Proof of habit of person generally, see 7 Am. Jur. Proof of Facts 2d 523, at 589. Proof of habitual behavior in crossing the street, see 7 Am. Jur. Proof of Facts 3d 523, at 567.

Handwriting

Elements

When authenticating a letter or other document, proof of handwriting can be crucial. These are the elements which must be proved: 1) the trial witness recognizes the handwriting and/or the signature on the exhibit; 2) the witness is shown to be familiar with the handwriting style either through business or social connections, or by other means; 3) the familiarity was not acquired for purposes of this litigation.

Direct Examination

Q. **(by plaintiff's attorney for Acme Manufacturing Company)**

Will you state your name, please?

A. Harold Turbyfill.

Q. What is your occupation?

A. Assembly supervisor at Acme Manufacturing.

Q. How long have you worked at the company?

A. Seven years. I have been the assembly supervisor since 1991, three years ago.

Q. As assembly supervisor, do you know Conrad X. Spindle?

A. Yes.

Q. How do you know him?

A. Conrad is the assistant supervisor on the small parts line. He has worked at the company for three years.

Q. During that period, have you seen his handwriting?

A. Yes, at least once a day. At the end of the shift, every assistant supervisor prepares a one page "Materials and Assembly Report" and signs it.

Q. Did you develop your knowledge of his handwriting especially for this lawsuit?

A. No. As I said, in our regular work pattern I see his handwritten reports, and his signature. Sometimes he has completed the "Materials and Assembly Report" in my presence.

Counsel: Your honor, I request that this document be marked for identification. **(After clerk does so)** Please let the record reflect that I am showing it to opposing counsel.

Court: The record will so show.

Counsel: Permission to approach the witness, your honor?

Court: Permission granted.

Q. I hand you what has been marked plaintiff's exhibit 3, which purports to be a written statement. Can you tell us in whose handwriting this statement appears?

A. That of Conrad Spindle.

Q. Will you please look at the signature: Do you have an opinion as to who signed this statement?

A. Conrad Spindle.

Q. Why do you say that?

A. The handwriting style in the body of the statement, and the signature, are all in Conrad's hand.

Counsel: Your honor, plaintiff offers plaintiff's exhibit three for identification into evidence as plaintiff's exhibit three in evidence.

Opposing Attorney: No objection.

Court: Exhibit received.

Counsel: Your honor, permission is requested to publish the exhibit by distributing it to the jurors for their inspection.

Court: Permission granted.

Rule Reference

Federal Evidence Rule 901. Requirement of Authentication or Identification. (a) General provision. The requirement of authentication or identification as a condition precedent to admissibility is satisfied by evidence sufficient to support a finding that the matter in question is what its proponent claims. *(b) Illustrations.* By way of illustration only, and not by way of limitation, the following are examples of authentication or identification conforming with the requirements of this rule:

. . . .

(2) Nonexpert opinion on handwriting. Nonexpert opinion as to the genuineness of handwriting, based upon familiarity not acquired for purposes of the litigation.

(3) Comparison by trier or expert witness. Comparison by the trier of fact or by expert witnesses with specimens which have been authenticated.

(4) Distinctive characteristics and the like. Appearance, contents, substance, internal patterns, or other distinctive characteristics, taken in conjunction with circumstances.

Cases and Authorities

See *United States v. Keene,* 341 F.3d 78, 84–85 (1st Cir. 2003)(stating that trier of fact was authorized to make handwriting comparison with or without expert testimony and holding no reversible error where prosecutor suggested jurors compare handwriting evidence on numbered labels from drug containers with samples of defendant's handwriting); *United States v. Scott,* 270 F.3d 30, 48 (1st Cir. 2001)(lay witness who acquired familiarity with defendant's handwriting in connection with IRS investigations can offer opinion testimony identifying defendant's handwriting).

Comment

Federal Evidence Rule 901 recognizes that a sufficient familiarity to authenticate another's writing may come from seeing him write, exchanging correspondence, or by additional means. "Testimony based upon familiarity acquired for purposes of the litigation is reserved to the expert...." Federal Advisory Committee's Note, Rule 901.

Handwriting identification may be the subject of lay witness proof as in the trial scene here, or by expert opinion.

It is generally held that anyone familiar with the handwriting of a given person may supply opinion testimony. Adequate familiarity may come from having seen the person write, or may result when the witness has seen writings purporting to be those of the person in question under circumstances indicating their genuineness. McCormick, Evidence § 221 (5th ed 1999).

Authentication is sometimes by circumstantial evidence as well. The special knowledge and the reply letter doctrines may be useful. R. Carlson, Successful Techniques for Civil Trials 2d § 4:35 (1992).

Experts may be called on the topic of handwriting or signatures, with the expert comparing the questioned handwriting with one or more genuine specimens. Carlson, supra.

Proofs for establishing questioned handwriting by means of expert testimony appear in 15 Am. Jur. Proof of Facts 3d 595.

Impeaching Own Witness

Elements

When counsel calls to the stand a witness who surprises her by reversing his testimony, counsel may need to impeach her own witness. These steps mark the process: 1) at first, proceed as though attempting to refresh the recollection of the witness; 2) if this is unsuccessful, have the witness' prior inconsistent statement marked for identification and confront the witness with it; 3) identify the date, place and person to whom the statement was made, and give the witness an opportunity to confirm that he made his statement to that person; 4) if the witness affirms that he made the statement, challenge him with the contradictory language; 5) on the other hand, if the witness continues to resist and reject his earlier account of the episode, the person to whom he made his statement will need to be called to authenticate it.

Direct Examination

In the hallway outside the courtroom, the witness assures the plaintiff's attorney that he will come through for the plaintiff in a car wreck case. "Look," he tells plaintiff's counsel, "I saw the whole thing and your guy—the driver of the silver Honda—had the green light." The witness is now called to the stand.

Q. Will you please state your name?

A. Willis X. Fortson.

Q. Where do you live?

A. 920 Madison Avenue in this city.

Q. What is your business or occupation?

A. Plumber. I have worked for Reliable Plumbing for 12 years.

Q. Going back to last June 12, do you remember something unusual that day?

A. Big accident. I was outside a job near the corner of Broad and High Streets, taking a break and having a smoke. I saw the whole thing.

Q. Could you please tell us what happened?

A. Sure. The silver Honda came from the east on Broad Street, approached the intersection at a high rate of speed, and ran the red light. Then the big crash with the black Cadillac.

Q. Mr. Fortson, I believe you may be mistaken as to the car which ran the red light. Wasn't it the black Cadillac?

A. No way. It was the silver Honda that blew the red light.

Q. Mr. Fortson, I now hand you a signed statement which has been marked. Will you please look at it?

A. Sure. **(witness does so)**

Q. Does that jog your memory about who ran the red light?

A. Well, it says at the top "Statement of Willis Fortson," and that is my signature at the bottom, but no, I still say it was the Honda that was in the wrong.

Q. You do recognize this statement as the one you signed in my office just one month after the wreck?

A. Yes.

Q. And you freely signed it, after describing the accident in your own words to my investigator?

A. Yes.

Q. Do you remember saying this, and for the record, I am reading from the second paragraph of the witness' prior statement: "The silver Honda waited for the green light, then went into the intersection real slow."

A. Let me see my writing. **(witness looks at Plaintiff's Exhibit 1 for identification)** Yes, I guess I did say exactly that.

Q. What statement was given closer to the time of the accident, your testimony today or the one you just read?

A. The one I just read, of course.

Plaintiff's Attorney: That's all.

Rule Reference

Federal Rule of Evidence 607 provides: The credibility of a witness may be attacked by any party, including the party calling the witness.

Cases and Authorities

Under the federal rule, liberal impeachment is permitted whenever a witness deserves it, whether or not the witness is called by the lawyer who proceeds to attack him. The current rule evolved by stages. Under earlier common law, court rules barred and completely disallowed impeaching one's own witness. The "no impeachment" rule was eroded when courts began allowing impeachment when the calling party was "surprised." Finally, the federal rule went further. It sets the pattern for modern federal and most state courts by eliminating the requirement of surprise entirely.

States no longer generally require the impeaching lawyer to be surprised, in order to impeach. However, in a few states which have enacted evidence codes based on the federal rules, the surprise requirement continues. See, e.g., Rule 607, Oh. R. Ev. (credibility of a witness may be attacked by the party calling the witness by means of prior inconsistent statement only upon showing of surprise and affirmative damage). On the other hand, some states without federal rules have eliminated the "surprise" doctrine by judicial fiat. See *Speed v. State*, 270 Ga. 688, 512 S.E.2d 896 (1999)(a party may impeach his or her own witness without a showing of surprise, notwithstanding a state statute which by its terms embraced the old rule and suggested that there should be no such impeachment unless the impeaching party can show that he "has been entrapped by said witness"). This line of cases demonstrates how modern court decisions sometimes override antiquated statutes like OCGA § 24–9–81 (Georgia).

Comment

Because a lawyer does not wish to appear to be on the attack against a witness she has called to the stand, her first effort will be to refresh the memory of a disappointing witness. If that does not work and it becomes apparent that the person is a true "turncoat," other measures are needed. That's when the impeachment mode enters the picture, as illustrated in this section's earlier Q. and A.

In addition to the scenario of impeaching one's own witness, another contingency occasions stern examination of a witness by the direct examiner. This is when she uses Federal Evidence Rule 611(c) to call and interrogate an adverse party. This latter situation is usually hostile from the outset and a cross-examination atmosphere prevails. Federal rules are not the only ones which permit this procedure. State rules also permit the calling and cross-examination of an adverse party. For example, a defendant in a civil case may be interrogated by leading questions when called during the plaintiff's case-in-chief. See OCGA § 24–9–81 (Georgia).

Insurance Information

Elements

Insurance information is generally inadmissible. However, there will be instances when an opponent's party admission carries a reference about the fact of insurance. In order to prove such an admission, counsel should establish the following things: 1) the witness heard one of the parties make a statement, and identifies the author of the remark; 2) the declaration is inconsistent with that party's position at trial; 3) the trial witness is called by one party **(party A)** and the declaration was uttered by the opposing party **(party B)**, either personally or through an agent; 4) even though insurance information is contained in the admission, the admission has relevance to an issue which is controverted and the insurance evidence is not injected simply to prejudice the case.

Direct Examination

Plaintiff decedent's estate has sued an agricultural services corporation over plaintiff's death in a grain elevator explosion.

Q. **(by plaintiff's attorney)** Mr. Scott, what is your position with Midwest and Pacific Grain Elevators Corporation?

A. I am—or was—the supervisor in charge of the Villa Peak elevator, until it exploded.

Q. Prior to the explosion, did you have a conversation with Howard Z. Laughlin?

A. Yes.

Q. Who is he?

A. Vice-president of the defendant corporation. Laughlin is in charge of grain elevator operations.

Q. Where and when did the conversation occur?

A. In Laughlin's office at the company's headquarters in Lincoln. This was about two weeks before the explosion. I was there expressing concern about potential fire and explosion hazards at the Villa Peak elevator. We had been near the flash point several times, and no ignition suppression devices had been installed by the company.

Q. What did Mr. Laughlin say?

Objection by Defense: Objection, insurance information.

Response by Plaintiff's Attorney: It has independent relevance, your honor.

Court: Overruled.

A. He told me not to worry about the Villa Peak operation, that if it blew up the company had a 5 million dollar policy on the operation with Wayne's of Liverpool insurers.

Q. Did the place explode?

A. About two weeks after the conversation I just mentioned.

The grain dust ignited, there was an explosion in the elevator, and several men were killed. Now we have these lawsuits over their wrongful deaths.

Rule References

Federal Rule of Evidence 801(d)(2)(A) provides that a statement is not hearsay if "[t]he statement is offered against a party and is (A) the party's own statement, in either an individual or a representative capacity."

Federal Rule of Evidence 411 states: "Evidence that a person was or was not insured against liability is not admissible upon the issue whether the person acted negligently or otherwise wrongfully. This rule does not require the exclusion of evidence of insurance against liability when offered for another purpose, such as proof of agency, ownership, or control, or bias or prejudice of a witness."

Cases and Authorities

It is well settled that an admission of liability is not rendered inadmissible by the fact that the jury may incidentally be apprised thereby that the defendant has liability insurance. *Nehring v. Smith*, 243 Iowa 225, 49 N.W.2d 831, 837 (1951). In *Reid v. Owens*, 98 Utah 50, 93 P.2d 680, 684–85 (1939), a similar result prevailed. In another case, prior to an accident a party who was later injured admonished the defendant to be careful with his driving. The defendant, who shortly thereafter turned his car over, responded: "Don't worry, I carry insurance for that." In the injured party's lawsuit, the remark was deemed admissible. *Herschensohn v. Weisman*, 80 N.H. 557, 119 A. 705 (1923)(citing law from Alabama, California, Montana, New Hampshire, South Dakota and Utah).

In 40 A.L.R. Fed 541 § 7 this statement appears: "It has been held that an admission of a party bearing on the issue of negligence or wrongdoing is admissible even though it contains a reference to liability insurance coverage."

Comment

Where a party's reply to another person's expression of concern references insurance and indicates indifference to consequences by stating "I carry insurance for that," case law often supports introduction of the admission into evidence. This can be particularly true where punitive damages and a wanton state of mind are alleged. For reference to admissions which carry insurance information into evidence, see 40 ALR Fed. 541 § 7; 4 ALR 2d 761.

Where the insurance reference can be easily separated from the remainder of the admission and the admission can stand alone, courts will sometimes insist upon redaction. See *Keown v. Monks*, 491 So.2d 914, 915–16 (Ala. 1986)("I've got insurance and I'm just real sorry").

In addition to the admissions rationale, there are other ways to admit insurance. Under Rule 411 there are a number of exceptions, such as bias. See *Ede v. Atrium South OB–GYN, Inc.*, 71 Ohio St.3d 124, 642 N.E.2d 365 (1994).

Absent special circumstances, insurance information is generally not admissible. *Pride Transport Co. v. Hughes*, 591 S.W.2d 631 (Tex. Civ. App. 1979)(rule rests upon fear that jury will decide case on improper basis). See *Palmer v. Krueger*, 897 F.2d 1529 (10th Cir. 1990).

Judicial Notice

Elements

Trial proof on a point will be excused when a party convinces the judge to judicially notice a fact. To accomplish this, apply these elements: 1) facts may be judicially noticed when they are undisputed or are not reasonably subject to dispute; 2) the judicially noticed facts must be generally known or capable of ready confirmation by "sources whose accuracy cannot reasonably be questioned."

Cross Examination

Often judicial notice is requested by a party during her case-in-chief. When taken by the judge, the party is relieved of the burden of producing additional evidence on that point. On some occasions, notice is requested upon cross-examination, as the following passage illustrates.

Q. (by plaintiff's attorney to a doctor who testified in an injury damages case for the defense) Doctor, you said that whiplash injuries are almost always baseless claims, invariably clearing up pretty much on their own in 4 to 8 weeks?

A. Yes.

Q. Are you familiar with *Wilfong's Manual of Cervical Injuries?*

A. Yes.

Q. Is it a standard in the field?

A. Not by me. I rarely refer to it.

Q. But it is a recognized text used by medical schools, isn't that correct?

A. Could be. I'm not sure.

Cross-examiner **(at bench)**: Your honor, please judicially notice the *Wilfong* text. In support of this request, I have a letter from the dean of the local medical school affirming that the *Wilfong* text *is the* standard work for diagnosis and treatment of cervical strain injuries. Here is that letter. In addition, I have a recent article in our State Medical Society's Monthly Journal of Medicine which takes the same position.

Court to Direct Examiner: Do you have any other evidence to dispute the text?

Direct Examiner: No, your honor. Not beyond that which you just heard.

Court: Request for judicial notice is granted.

Q. **(by cross examiner)** Doctor, how do you square your opinion with this passage on page 357 of *Wilfong*: "Many cases of reversal of normal cervical curve are severe, with disability extending for several years"?

Rule References

Federal Evidence Rule 201(b). Kinds of facts. A judicially noticed fact must be one not subject to reasonable dispute in that it is either (1) generally known within the territorial jurisdiction of the trial court or (2) capable of accurate and ready determination by resort to sources whose accuracy cannot reasonably be questioned.

Rule 803(18) pertaining to learned treatises, is set forth at the *Texts and Treatises* entry, infra.

Cases and Authorities

A commonly invoked technique of establishing a fact is judicial notice. The judge notes the existence of a fact and

instructs the jury that the fact exists. Judicial notice expedites
the trial by dispensing with the formal proof of the fact. R.
Carlson, E. Imwinkelried, E. Kionka and K. Strachan, Evidence: Teaching Materials for an Age of Science and Statutes
33 (5th ed. 2002). Some facts are well known and beyond any
serious dispute. Others are easily verified by resort to reliable
sources. This is where judicial notice comes in, to obviate the
need for formal proof of the fact. See *York v. American Tel. &
Tel. Co.*, 95 F.3d 948 (10th Cir. 1996)(judicial notice is adjudi-
cative device that alleviates parties' evidentiary duties at trial,
serving as substitute for conventional method of taking evidence to establish facts).

Stock and securities litigation has sometimes led to requests
for judicial notice. See *La Grasta v. First Union Secs., Inc.*,
358 F.3d 840 (11th Cir. 2004)(taking judicial notice of Ask
Jeeves stock on days during period in question, noting prices
not subject to reasonable dispute and topic was proper subject
for judicial notice); *In re Towne Services, Inc. Securities Litigation*, 184 F.Supp.2d 1308, 1312 (N.D. Ga. 2001)(court took
judicial notice of filings with the Securities and Exchange
Commission).

Taking judicial notice of the harm that prostitution activity
has on a neighborhood, see *City of Milwaukee v. Burnette*, 248
Wis.2d 820, 637 N.W.2d 447 (Wis. App. 2001). One commenta-
tor opposes decisions in criminal cases which have allowed
trial courts to take binding judicial notice of jurisdiction and
venue, see W. Carter, "Trust Me, I'm a Judge": Why Binding
Judicial Notice of Jurisdictional Facts Violates the Rights to
Jury Trial, 68 Mo. L. Rev. 649 (2003).

Comment

In deciding whether or not to judicially notice a matter, the
court can factor into its decision information from a number
of sources. The court in the foregoing Q. and A. example uses
a representation from a local medical dean as well as a

reference from a respected and well-known journal within the jurisdiction. On the inquiry into whether to take judicial notice, the court is not bound by the hearsay rule or formal rules of evidence. The judicially noticed fact—the standard character of a text—was verified by two reliable sources.

Dispensing with traditional methods of proof will be done by the court only in clear cases. Rule 201 of the Federal Rules of Evidence is the dominant provision in the rules detailing judicial notice. Rule 803(18) references judicial notice in the context of the trial proof demonstrated here, impeachment by a scientific text. Judicial notice of authoritative treatise to impeach an expert, see 31 Am. Jur. Proof of Facts 2d 443, at §§ 7, 8. Establishing the law of another jurisdiction, see 21 Am. Jur. Proof of Facts 2d 1.

Juror Misconduct

Elements

On a motion for new trial, a losing party can endeavor to overturn the jury's verdict if there were indications after the trial of juror misconduct. To establish such misconduct in an affidavit or by live juror testimony, the following points should be made: 1) during the trial or deliberations, someone approached a juror and pressured or threatened him; or, material not brought out at trial came before the jurors during deliberations; 2) this extraneous information or outside influence prejudiced the jury in its decision.

Direct Examination

Q. **(by defense attorney at a hearing on his motion for new trial)** Ms. Walker, were you a juror in the case decided in this court last week in which the jury rendered a verdict against the defendant?

A. Yes.

Q. On the weekend prior to the Monday when the jury decided the case, did you and your husband do anything related to the case?

A. Yes. We took a drive to where the accident had happened.

Q. Did you drive by, or did you stop?

A. We stopped. I got out, then he backed up the roadway and began testing stopping distances.

Q. How many times did he do this?

A. Nine or ten times.

Q. Did he explain why he was conducting all these tests?

A. Yes. The defendant driver claimed to have been going only 25 m.p.h. and to have hit her brakes at the point where I paced it off. My husband wanted to see if that would stop you before you crossed into the intersection, at that speed.

Q. Did he explain to you what his findings were?

A. Yes, he said the defendant must be lying.

Q. What did your husband do next?

A. We went home and he prepared a diagram setting out what we had discovered at the scene of the accident. It was on a yellow pad page.

Q. What did you do with the diagram, if anything?

A. I folded it up and put it in my purse. When the jury was deliberating on the case, I brought it out and showed it to the other jurors.

Rule Reference

Federal Evidence Rule 606(b). Inquiry into validity of verdict or indictment. Upon an inquiry into the validity of a verdict or indictment, a juror may not testify as to any matter or statement occurring during the course of the jury's deliberations or to the effect of anything upon that or any other juror's mind or emotions as influencing the juror to assent to or dissent from the verdict or indictment or concerning the juror's mental processes in connection therewith, except that a juror may testify on the question whether extraneous prejudicial information was improperly brought to the jury's attention or whether any outside influence was improperly brought to bear upon any juror. Nor may a juror's affidavit or evidence of any statement by the juror concerning a matter about which the juror would be precluded from testifying be received for these purposes.

Cases and Authorities

See *Sassounian v. Roe*, 230 F.3d 1097, 1108 (9th Cir. 2000)(in deciding motion for a new trial, court can consider juror discussion of telephone call that was not admitted into evidence); *Powell v. Allstate Ins. Co.*, 652 So.2d 354 (Fla. 1995); *Hammock v. State*, 277 Ga. 612, 592 S.E.2d 415 (2004))(juror made measurements on her own, and after reporting her findings to the rest of the jury, a unanimous verdict was achieved; verdict overturned by Georgia Supreme Court). Denying relief based upon claims of juror misconduct, see *Tanner v. United States*, 483 U.S. 107, 107 S.Ct. 2739, 97 L.Ed.2d 90 (1987)(not "outside influence"); *United States v. Lanas*, 324 F.3d 894, 903–04 (7th Cir. 2003)(finding no error where spectator who was privy to proceedings not intended for jury and who accompanied juror to court each day testified that the two never discussed trial); *Newson v. Foster*, 261 Ga.App. 16, 581 S.E.2d 666 (2003)(jury based verdict in part on fact that jury foreman took it upon himself to visit the scene of an accident in a civil case, do his own investigation, and report back to rest of jury; Court of Appeals refused to extend to this civil case the criminal case rule which allows proof that jurors considered extraneous evidence, in order to overturn a tainted jury verdict).

Comment

Motions for new trial are of high practical significance, and where the new trial is sought on account of juror misconduct, it is quite justified. Forms for such motions as well as supporting affidavits and live testimony appear in R. Carlson, Successful Techniques for Civil Trials §§ 8:33—8:35 and 8:37–38.

During a trial, can a juror who is sitting on a case leave the jury box, take the witness stand and testify, then return as a juror? A juror may not testify as a witness in a case in which the juror is sitting, under the federal rule. Upon a motion for new trial, however, the juror is competent to testify to limited subjects. Thus, a juror may testify, upon an inquiry into a verdict, that extraneous prejudicial information was improperly brought to the jury's attention. A juror in such a proceeding may also testify that outside influence was improperly brought to bear upon a juror. Jury misconduct warranting a new trial, including whether reading newspaper accounts concerning the trial prejudiced the case, is discussed in 24 Am. Jur. Proof of Facts 2d 633. Tests conducted by jurors and preparation of diagram of scene, see 24 Am. Jur. Proof of Facts 2d 633, at § 20.

Life Expectancy

Elements

To invoke a table which provides a projected lifespan for a party, the following requirements apply: 1) life expectancy is relevant to the case; 2) the proponent of a standard and accepted table will usually be able to secure judicial notice of it; 3) alternatively, a properly qualified expert may testify as to the probable duration of human life.

Direct Examination

In an injury case, the plaintiff's attorney interrogates in a manner which implicates the expected lifespan of his client.

Q. **(by plaintiff's attorney)** Doctor, how long will this pain continue for the plaintiff?

A. The remainder of his life.

Plaintiff's Attorney: Your honor, on the issue of life expectancy I respectfully request that the court judicially notice this standard mortality table marked plaintiff's exhibit one, drawn from vital statistics compiled by the U.S. National Center for Health Statistics.

Court: It will be received.

Rule Reference

Federal Evidence Rule 201 provides for judicial notice of facts not subject to reasonable dispute which are capable of accurate and ready determination by sources whose accuracy cannot reasonably be questioned.

Cases and Authorities

See *McAsey v. United States Dep't of Navy*, 201 F.Supp.2d 1081, 1097 (N.D. Cal. 2002)(noting that mortality table not conclusive evidence of life expectancy, but court may take judicial notice of standard mortality table to be considered with other relevant factors, such as the plaintiff's health and physical condition before he was injured, the hazards of his occupation, and his eating, drinking and smoking habits); *Mealey v. Slaton Mach. Sales, Inc.*, 508 F.2d 87 (5th Cir. 1975)(court allowed an economist to testify from certain government tables as to the work life expectancy of the deceased, and to compute his lifetime earnings based thereon with an assumed annual increase in his pay of 4%; held, the tables were admissible, and the court did not err in allowing the witness to refer to them).

A case which illustrates use of tables is *Reiser v. United States*, 786 F.Supp. 1334 (N.D. Ill. 1992). In a death case, survivors claimed a pilot died as a result of negligence on the part of FAA air traffic control personnel. Future life expectancy was a factor in the damage award calculation: "In making its damages determination, the court has employed the life expectancy table issued by the U.S. Department of Health and Human Services, which was contained in Plaintiff's Exhibit 42. Mortality tables are admissible in wrongful death actions on the subject of both the decedent's and the next of kin's life expectancy."

Comment

Generally courts take judicial notice of standard mortality tables as some evidence of the probable duration of human life. Many states by statute provide that standard mortality tables are admissible in evidence, and the Commissioners' Standard Ordinary Mortality Table has been printed in numerous state code compilations. Details on proving life expectancy are contained in 7 Am. Jur. Proof of Facts 215; R.

Carlson, Successful Techniques for Civil Trials 2d §§ 3:18–3:20. One life expectancy table may be found at Am. Jur. 2d Desk Book, Item No. 92, reprinted in R. Carlson, supra at § 3:20. On the topic of judicial notice, see in this text *Judicial Notice*.

Medical Causation

Elements

When an expert is interrogated, it is frequently imperative to link the litigated incident **(assault, auto wreck, slip-and-fall injury)** to the plaintiff's disabled physical condition. This is accomplished in the following fashion: 1) calling and qualifying a medical expert; 2) establish the doctor's examination and **(where applicable)** course of treatment of the patient; 3) ask the expert whether the physical disability or illness came from plaintiff's involvement in the litigated event.

Direct Examination

Plaintiff's Attorney: Doctor, do you have an opinion, based upon a reasonable degree of medical probability, as to whether the accident caused these conditions?

Q. Yes. I have an opinion.

A. What is that opinion?

Objection: Your honor, speculative, the doctor is not certain, and certainty is required. Thus, the question asks for an opinion based on mere probability, which is insufficient causal connection.

Court: Overruled.

Plaintiff's Attorney: Please state your opinion as to causation, Doctor.

A. It is highly likely that the plaintiff's condition was directly attributable to the accident. I believe the accident was the probable cause of his disability.

Rule Reference

Federal Rule 702. Testimony by Experts. If scientific, technical, or other specialized knowledge will assist the trier of fact to understand the evidence or to determine a fact in issue, a witness qualified as an expert by knowledge, skill, experience, training, or education, may testify thereto in the form of an opinion or otherwise, if (1) the testimony is based upon sufficient facts or data, (2) the testimony is the product of reliable principles and methods, and (3) the witness has applied the principles and methods reliably to the facts of the case.

Cases and Authorities

Soldo v. Sandoz Pharmals. Corp., 244 F.Supp.2d 434, 524–25 (W.D. Pa. 2003)(describing requirements that plaintiff meet medical causation burden by first establishing general causation, that drug was capable of causing plaintiff's injury, then specific causation, that drug in fact caused plaintiff's injury, to a reasonable degree of medical certainty); *Kennedy v. Southern California Edison Co.*, 268 F.3d 763, 768 (9th Cir. 2001)(under California law, causation must be proven within a reasonable medical probability based on competent expert testimony); *Glastetter v. Novartis Pharmaceuticals Corp.*, 252 F.3d 986, 992 (8th Cir. 2001)(district court properly excluded expert testimony that did not demonstrate causation to an acceptable degree of medical certainty).

Comment

In developing expert testimony, two levels of connection and projection are important. They deal with whether an initial accident caused the plaintiff's current disability, and the future course of the impairment. On the first issue regarding the current condition of the plaintiff, in order to make an issuable case, the courtroom expert will attribute the plaintiff's medical condition to the accident, explosion or other litigated incident. Causal connection may be established by: (1) reasonable medical certainty; (2) medical probability; or (3) (in some courts) a possibility. If the connective proof is by possibility only, it must be coupled with lay testimony that the injured party did not suffer from the malady prior to the accident, but now is afflicted with the condition.

When *future* injuries are sought to be established, the second question raised in the preceding paragraph, a higher level of conviction may be called for than is the case with the initial connective proof. A prognosis of future pain will require the expert to be reasonably certain, in many states; some courts sustain an award for future damages when there is a reasonable probability **(as opposed to certainty)** that future damage will occur.

Related matter, see the topics *Pathologist's Opinion, Qualifications of Expert, and Medical History* in this text.

Medical History

Elements

When a plaintiff's doctor testifies on behalf of the plaintiff in a personal injury case, it is often persuasive for the jury to hear what the plaintiff told his doctor. The physician should be asked questions designed to bring out the plaintiff's earlier declarations to his doctor, as follows: 1) the declaration was made to medical personnel, or to another person for purposes of transmission to a doctor or other healer; 2) the statement was made by the declarant for purposes of diagnosis or treatment of the patient's condition.

Direct Examination

Q. **(by plaintiff's attorney)** Will you please give us your name?

A. Dr. Darla Wilson.

Q. Will you please state your qualifications?

A. After graduating from Duke Medical School, I interned at Emory Hospital. I was a resident at Northwestern Hospitals in Chicago, specializing in family medicine. I have practiced medicine in this city for four years, and am on the staff of two local hospitals.

Q. Have you published any writings?

A. Yes, my forthcoming article in the *International Journal of Orthodox Medicine* is entitled "Neck Injuries and the Family Practitioner."

Q. Do you know the plaintiff?

A. Yes, I met him at the hospital. I was getting ready to treat him for his injuries.

Q. Will you please describe his condition?

A. When he first came into the emergency room he was in a great deal of pain.

Q. Doctor, did you take a history from my client?

A. Yes.

Q. Did you ask about the cause of pain?

Objection by Defense: Hearsay.

Plaintiff's Counsel: Your honor, items of history relevant to current condition of the patient and his treatment are admissible as an exception to the hearsay rule. Rule 803(4), Federal Rules of Evidence, provides that statements for purposes of medical diagnosis or treatment and describing history are proper subjects of testimony by the doctor.

Court: Overruled.

Plaintiff's Counsel: Did the patient mention the cause of the pain?

A. Yes. He said that he received a severe blow to his head, that his head was struck very hard, and that he was thrown head-first through the windshield when another car collided with his own.

Rule Reference

Federal Evidence Rule 803. Hearsay Exceptions; Availability of Declarant Immaterial. The following are not excluded by the hearsay rule, even though the declarant is available as a witness:

. . .

(4) Statements for purpose of medical diagnosis or treatment. Statements made for purposes of medical diagnosis or

treatment and describing medical history, or past or present symptoms, pain, or sensations, or the inception or general character of the cause or external source thereof insofar as reasonably pertinent to diagnosis or treatment.

Cases and Authorities

See *United States v. Wright,* 340 F.3d 724, 732–33 (8th Cir. 2003)(holding there was sufficient foundation to conclude statements by patient to emergency room doctor regarding incidents of past seven days were for purposes of medical diagnosis or treatment, and noting that statements must be pertinent to or kind reasonably relied on for treatment or diagnosis); *Swinton v. Potomac Corp.,* 270 F.3d 794, 808 (9th Cir. 2001)(district court properly admitted psychologist's rendition of patient's medical history).

In *United States v. Edward J.,* 224 F.3d 1216 (10th Cir. 2000), the Tenth Circuit Court of Appeals held that statements made by two children during a medical examination that were later repeated by the physician at trial were admissible as medical history hearsay. Two young girls told a physician during a medical examination that they had been sexually molested by their uncle. The uncle was prosecuted by the United States, and the physician testified about the girls' statements. At trial, both girls' testified and their testimony was consistent with their comments to the physician. Defendant was found guilty. Affirming, the Tenth Circuit held that the rationale behind Fed. R. Evid. 803(4), which allows the admission of hearsay statements made to a physician, is that because a patient's medical care depends on the accuracy of the information provided to the physician, the patient has a selfish motive to be truthful, and such statements are consequently deemed reliable.

Comment

Statements to hospital attendants, ambulance drivers, or even members of the family may be included in the exception, when it is intended that they be passed on to the treating physician. The courts realize that when the declarant knows that his description of symptoms will affect his treatment, his realization is a strong motive for sincerity. R. Carlson, E. Imwinkelried, E. Kionka & K. Strachan, Evidence: Teaching Materials for an Age of Science and Statutes 498 (5th ed 2002). A statement as to cause of an injury is proper but not a statement assigning fault to another, since the declarant's statement must be "reasonably pertinent to diagnosis or treatment."

Offer of Compromise

Elements

When a party is negotiating with an opposing side and trying to settle his case, he should be able to speak freely and not worry about frank and candid comments being later used against him. To exclude such remarks from a later trial, the objecting party needs to establish the following: 1) a valuable consideration was offered by party B to compromise the opposing party's disputed claim (claim of party A); 2) party A attempts to prove liability against B by establishing that B offered to settle the case; 3) A's proof that an offer of compromise was made will be excluded, as well as any admissions by B "made in compromise negotiations."

Direct Examination

Q. **(by plaintiff's attorney)** Officer, after the defendant left the scene of the accident and between that time and now, did you see the defendant again?

A. Yes.

Q. Where?

A. The day after the wreck, March 31, I went to the plaintiff's room at Mercy Hospital to complete my notes on the case.

Q. Officer, did you see the defendant at the hospital?

A. Yes, he came to the plaintiff's room and told the plaintiff he was sorry.

Q. What else did he say, if anything?

Defense Attorney: Objection. Brief voire dire, your honor? Thank you. Officer, now that we are outside of the jury's presence, tell us what my client said to the plaintiff there at the hospital?

A. Defendant said he felt like hell about the whole thing because he had run the red light, but not to worry, that for a release of claims, he would prepay all medical and hospital expenses and would take care of any lost wages by the plaintiff.

Defense Attorney: Defense objects to the plaintiff's request that this officer relate the hospital conversation in front of the jury, your honor. Offer of compromise.

Court: Sustained.

Rule Reference

Federal Evidence Rule 408. Compromise and Offers to Compromise. Evidence of (1) furnishing or offering or promising to furnish, or (2) accepting or offering or promising to accept, a valuable consideration in compromising or attempting to compromise a claim which was disputed as to either validity or amount, is not admissible to prove liability for or invalidity of the claim or its amount. Evidence of conduct or statements made in compromise negotiations is likewise not admissible. This rule does not require the exclusion of any evidence otherwise discoverable merely because it is presented in the course of compromise negotiations. This rule also does not require exclusion when the evidence is offered for another purpose, such as proving bias or prejudice of a witness, negativing a contention of undue delay, or proving an effort to obstruct a criminal investigation or prosecution.

Cases and Authorities

See *Pacific Gas & Elec. Co. v. Lynch*, 216 F.Supp.2d 1016, 1026 (N.D. Cal. 2002)(noting one underlying principle of Fed.

R. Evid. 408, that "evidence of a settlement is generally not relevant, because settlements may be motivated by a variety of factors unrelated to liability"); *United States v. Logan*, 250 F.3d 350, 366–67 (6th Cir. 2001)(Federal Rule of Evidence 408 barring admission of offers of compromise does not always prohibit admission of administrative negotiations which occurred in a criminal context); *Coleman v. Quaker Oats Co.*, 232 F.3d 1271, 1290–91 (9th Cir. 2000)(district court properly excluded settlement offer).

Comment

Rule 408 of the Federal Rules of Evidence bars offers of compromise, subject to limited exceptions provided for in the rule. The Federal Rules of Evidence also prohibit proof of offers to pay medical expenses. See Rule 409 (but protection for incidental factual statements is not as broad as in Rule 408). Finally, Rule 410 extends exclusionary protection to pleas of guilty which are later withdrawn, as well as to statements made while plea bargaining with a prosecutor. In a criminal case, defense counsel may object, perhaps at the bench: "Objection, your honor, question seeks evidence of statements made during a plea proceeding."

Admissions separated from negotiation discussions, those made at a separate time and place, are admissible. In certain cases, so is the fact that parties were engaged in lengthy good-faith settlement negotiations. This fact may become relevant in a case where one of them later claims that the opposing party delayed resolution of the case simply to obstruct justice. For the most part, however, offers of compromise are inadmissible, as are offers to pay medical expenses.

Accordingly, it is valuable to be able to prove the fact that otherwise damaging admissions were made in the context of settlement negotiations. In addition to authorities in this section of the text, see Annotation, Admissibility of evidence to show payment or offer or promise of payment of medical, hospital, and similar expenses of an injured party by the opposing party, 65 ALR 3d 932. Compromise offers, *Proof of Facts* reference, see 32 Am. Jur. Proof of Facts 2d 253, at § 8.

Offer of Proof

Elements

This device is an essential one for making a proper record of trial court proceedings. An offer of proof proceeds as follows: 1) counsel is interrogating a witness and the judge sustains an objection to the witness' testimony; 2) the court's ruling on the evidentiary point will normally not be appealable in the absence of an offer of proof; 3) the offer contains a recital of the evidence which the proponent expected to present.

Direct Examination

Q. As an experienced highway patrol officer, were you able to isolate the point of impact between the two vehicles, in your opinion?

A. Yes.

Q. Where was it?

Objection by opponent. Improper subject for expert opinion.

Court: Sustained.

Proponent of witness: Your honor, I would like to make an offer of proof on that.

Court: Approach the bench. Ms. Reporter, please approach also.

Proponent of witness: Let the record show that if Officer Cahalan had testified to point of impact, he would have placed it about 6 feet south of the center line, in the plaintiff's lane of travel. Please let the record further show that plaintiff contends that such point-of-impact testimony from a qualified witness has been approved by the supreme court of this state.

Rule Reference

Federal Evidence Rule 103. Rulings on Evidence. (a) Effect of erroneous ruling. Error may not be predicated upon a ruling which admits or excludes evidence unless a substantial right of the party is affected, and *(1) Objection.* In case the ruling is one admitting evidence, a timely objection or motion to strike appears of record, stating the specific ground of objection, if the specific ground was not apparent from the context; or *(2) Offer or Proof.* In case the ruling is one excluding evidence, the substance of the evidence was made known to the court by offer or was apparent from the context within which questions were asked. . . .

Cases and Authorities

The critical role of an effective offer of proof is emphasized in *United States v. Rettenberger*, 344 F.3d 702, 706 (7th Cir. 2003)(stating that defense counsel's failure to make offer of proof after district court blocked defense witness's testimony "scuttle[d] [defendant's] position" on appeal because the substance of potential testimony was not known). See *Tiller v. Baghdady*, 244 F.3d 9, 14 (1st Cir. 2001)(oral offer of proof, even though never put in writing, adequately preserved issue of whether exclusion of evidence was error).

Comment

There are a number of ways to make the offer of proof, and factors which justify the failure to accomplish this step when appellate court questions are asked about the absence of an offer, upon appeal. These are chronicled in R. Carlson, Successful Techniques for Civil Trials 2d § 2:37 (1992).

Prior to trial, a party may be on the losing side of a judicial decision to exclude evidence. If a motion in limine adjudicates that a party cannot introduce specified trial proof, an offer of proof by the losing party will protect the record for appeal. Must the party *repeat* the offer at trial? No, is the usual answer to this question, at least where the judge firmly ruled against the party in the motion hearing and the losing party made a satisfactory offer. See *United States v. McGauley*, 279 F.3d 62, 72 (1st Cir. 2002)(once the court makes a definitive ruling on the record admitting or excluding evidence, either at or before trial, a party need not renew an objection or offer of proof to preserve a claim of error on appeal).

Opinion by Lay Witness

Elements

While lay witnesses usually testify in a factual format, there are special topics which merit opinions from nonexpert witnesses. The following factors justify lay opinion: 1) a lay witness has first hand knowledge of the facts; 2) the witness has an opinion about a relevant issue; 3) it would be difficult for the lay witness to identify all of the component details that support the opinion, and this difficulty justifies the conclusory format; 4) the opinion is on a topic which is regularly the subject of lay opinion.

Direct Examination

Q. Mr. Jones, were you in a position to see the defendant's car?

A. Yes. I was driving my car south on highway 51 when the defendant passed me; this was about a half-mile before the wreck.

Q. Will you please describe what you saw?

A. The defendant came around me at a rapid rate of speed, then continued to pull away until the point of collision. He was way ahead of me when the wreck happened.

Q. Did you form an opinion as to the defendant's speed?

A. Yes.

Q. Will you tell the jury the speed you believe the defendant was traveling when he pulled around you?

A. Between 60 and 65 miles per hour.

Rule Reference

Federal Evidence Rule 701. Opinion Testimony by Lay Witnesses. If the witness is not testifying as an expert, the witness' testimony in the form of opinions or inferences is limited to those opinions or inferences which are (a) rationally based on the perception of the witness and (b) helpful to a clear understanding of the witness' testimony or the determination of a fact in issue, and (c) not based on scientific, technical, or other specialized knowledge within the scope of rule 702.

Cases and Authorities

Mississippi Chemical Corp. v. Dresser–Rand Co., 287 F.3d 359, 373–74 (5th Cir. 2002)(permitting opinion testimony concerning company's lost profits by lay witness with personal knowledge of company's books); *Harms v. Laboratory Corp. of Am.*, 155 F.Supp.2d 891, 904 (N.D. Ill. 2001)(permitting lay witness opinion testimony of general standard of care in industry). See also *Tampa Bay Shipbuilding & Repair Co. v. Cedar Shipping Co.*, 320 F.3d 1213, 1223 (11th Cir. 2003)(determining that testimony by company employees that charges as well as ship repair time were reasonable was admissible because testimony was type traditionally considered lay witness testimony, not based on specialized knowledge, and helpful to the district judge).

Clause (c) was added to Rule 701 in December, 2000. The Advisory Committee Notes which accompanied the 2000 amendment to Rule 701 explained that subsection (c) was an attempt "to eliminate the risk that the reliability requirements set forth in Rule 702 will be evaded through the simple expedient of proffering an expert in lay witness clothing." The Notes also explained that the amendment was not intended to affect the "prototypical example[s] of the type of evidence contemplated by the adoption of Rule 701 relat[ing] to the appearance of persons or things, identity, the manner of conduct, competency of a person, degrees of light or darkness, sound, size, weight, distance, and an endless number of items that cannot be described factually in words apart from inferences." Fed. R. Evid. 701 Advisory Committee's Note (citing *Asplundh Mfg. Div. v. Benton Harbor Eng'g,* 57 F.3d 1190, 1196 (3d Cir. 1995)).

Comments

There are certain opinions that lay witnesses commonly and reliably form. Thus, on some subjects it is clearer for the trier of fact to receive opinion testimony from the lay witness, rather than a tortured attempt to detail numerous component facts. Inferences that lay witnesses are allowed to draw include opinions as to intoxication of an observed person, speed of vehicles, voice and handwriting identification, the state of emotion of another person, whether the speech or acts of a person seemed rational or irrational, and identity of an individual. Lay opinion on testamentary capacity is developed in 18 Am. Jur. Proof of Facts 2d 1. Lay opinion on intoxication, testamentary capacity and handwriting, see R. Carlson, Successful Techniques for Civil Trials 2d §§ 4:16–4:18 (1992).

Pathologist's Opinion

Elements

Testimony from a pathologist about the cause and manner of death can be important. To elicit it, the lawyer should show that: 1) the witness is qualified as an expert in pathology; qualifications include educational background, medical licenses, publications, medical society memberships, awards and honors, number of deaths investigated, autopsies performed, and the like; 2) the expert has a reliable basis for her opinion, as by examination of the body or study of the records in the case, interviews, or a combination of the above; 3) an opinion is given by the expert on a relevant issue in the case.

Direct Examination

Q. Doctor, do you have a specialty?

A. Yes, forensic pathology.

Q. Could you tell us what forensic pathology is, doctor?

A. Yes. Pathology is the study of human tissues and fluids.

We identify the causes of disease and death. Forensic pathology is concerned primarily with certain kinds of cases, including unexplained or suspicious deaths. Some of these, of course, result from criminal causes.

Q. What investigation did you make in this case?

A. I conducted an autopsy on the deceased. An autopsy is a complete examination of the organs and tissues of the deceased.

Q. What did you find?

A. This 18–year-old male had been found hanging from an overhead pipe in the Dover County jail. I examined the body at Dover Paramount Hospital shortly after he was found and taken there. The tongue protruded, or stuck out, from the mouth and the tip had dried. There were no indicators of internal damage from blows or traumatic causes, and no such indications externally. I noted an absence of bruises, scratches, abrasions, things of that kind.

Q. Doctor, based upon your training and experience and your external and internal examination of the body of the deceased, do you have an opinion based upon a reasonable degree of medical certainty of the cause of death of this person?

A. Yes.

Q. Will you please give us your opinion, doctor?

A. The deceased expired as a result of asphyxia due to hanging.

Rule References

Federal Evidence Rule 702. Testimony by Experts. If scientific, technical, or other specialized knowledge will assist the trier of fact to understand the evidence or to determine a fact in issue, a witness qualified as an expert by knowledge, skill, experience, training, or education, may testify thereto in the form of an opinion or otherwise.

Federal Evidence Rule 703. Bases of Opinion Testimony by Experts. The facts or data in the particular case upon which an expert bases an opinion or inference may be those perceived by or made known to the expert at or before the hearing. If of a type reasonably relied upon by experts in the particular field in forming opinions or inferences upon the subject, the facts or data need not be admissible in evidence.

Cases and Authorities

Testimony by a pathologist can play an important role in civil as well as criminal cases. See *Smith v. BMW N. Am., Inc.*, 308 F.3d 913, 919–20 (8th Cir. 2002)(holding forensic pathologist's testimony as to how motorist sustained neck injury admissible where pathologist reached opinion by applying his medical knowledge and experience to the physical evidence, even though experts in other fields could also have testified regarding how injury occurred based on different factors); *Globetti v. Sandoz Pharmaceuticals, Corp.*, 111 F.Supp.2d 1174, 1179–80 (N.D. Ala. 2000)(admitting testimony of cardiac pathologist).

Comment

The Q. and A. trial proof earlier in this section is necessarily abbreviated because of space limitations. Treatment in an asphyxiation death of topics such as hemorrhages in the eyes, congestion of the lungs, and the like may be provided in specific cases in an expanded fashion.

Autopsy to determine cause of death, see 39 Am. Jur. Proof of Facts 2d 1. Qualification of medical expert witness, see 33 Am. Jur. Proof of Facts 2d 179.

Personal Opinion of Character

Elements

Unlike reputation proof, this mode of supporting or attacking character turns on the witness' personal knowledge of the party, not his appraisal of community impressions. The opinion character witness will be asked: 1) if he is personally acquainted with the party about whom he is testifying; 2) whether they know each other well enough for the witness to have developed a trustworthy opinion of the other party's character; 3) the trait of character inquired about is relevant to the case; 4) the witness states her opinion.

Direct Examination

Defendant Clarence Z. Douglas is charged with felony assault in State v Douglas. The defense attorney calls a friend of the defendant to the stand.

Q. Who is Mr. Douglas?

A. A friend of mine from work.

Q. Where do you and he work?

A. Bedford Bowling Supply Company.

Q. Do you see him in the courtroom?

A. Yes. He is seated right there **(witness points out defendant)**.

Q. Will you please describe his clothing?

A. (witness does so)

Defense Attorney: Your honor, will the record please show that the witness pointed out the defendant, Clarence Douglas.

Court: The record will so reflect.

Q. How long have you and he worked together at Bedford Bowling?

A. Three years.

Q. How often do you see Mr. Douglas?

A. Every day, five or six days a week.

Q. How well do you know him?

A. Very well. We work together on assembly at the job, so we are together for eight hours every work day.

Q. Are there any additional contacts by you with Mr. Douglas?

A. Yes. We bowl together on the company's bowling team.

That's two nights a week, and we have done that for at least a couple of years.

Q. Have you ever seen him in situations which might be termed tense or stressful?

A. Many times. Work deadlines impose those conditions on us regularly.

Q. Do you have an opinion as to whether he is a peaceful person?

A. Yes.

Q. What is your opinion?

A. Clarence Douglas is a very peaceful person. He is even tempered and not given to violence at all.

Rule Reference

Federal Evidence Rule 405. Methods of Proving Character.

(a) Reputation or Opinion. In all cases in which evidence of character or a trait of character of a person is admissible, proof may be made by testimony as to reputation or by

testimony in the form of an opinion. On cross-examination, inquiry is allowable into relevant specific instances.

Cases and Authorities

The traditional common law view rejected personal opinions of character, in favor of limiting character proof to reputation only. In the view of legal commentators, a view which was persuasive on the Federal Rules Advisory Committee, opinion proof should be deemed at least equally trustworthy as reputation evidence. In the end, the Federal Evidence Rules embraced both opinion and reputation as acceptable modes of proving character.

Federal Rule 405 implicitly rejects specific instances of conduct to prove character.

Comment

Under Federal Evidence Rule 404(a)(1) the defendant in a criminal case has the option of opening up the character issue, or leaving it closed. Customarily, the defendant opens the issue by calling a witness to give reputation or opinion testimony regarding the defendant's good character. R. Carlson, E. Imwinkelried, E. Kionka & K. Strachan, Evidence: Teaching Materials for an Age of Science and Statutes 318 (5th ed. 2002). In the foregoing Q. and A., the defendant has opened the issue by presenting an opinion witness to swear to the defendant's nonviolent nature.

Related topic, see *Character and Reputation: Violence and Peacefulness* in this text.

Photographs

Elements

To introduce photographs, develop these elements: 1) a trial witness is familiar with the person, object or scene which appears on the photograph; 2) the witness authenticates the photograph by stating that the photo is a true and correct representation of the scene or object portrayed in the photo.

Direct Examination

Plaintiff's Attorney: Your honor, I call the wife of the plaintiff to the stand.

Q. Will you please state your name?

A. Pat Johnson Jacobs.

Q. Are you married to the plaintiff, John Jacobs?

A. Yes.

Q. I show you a photograph which has previously been marked plaintiff's exhibit 1 for identification and ask whether or not you can identify it?

A. Yes I can.

Q. What is it?

A. A picture of my husband in the emergency right after the wreck. I was there with him.

Q. Is it a true accurate photograph of your husband as you saw him that night?

A. Yes.

Plaintiff's Attorney: I offer the plaintiff's Exhibit #1 into evidence.

Objection by Defendant: Inflammatory and prejudicial. This photo is gory.

Plaintiff's Attorney: May I be heard? Thank you. This exhibit illustrates the extent of plaintiff's injuries. The defense denies their severity, and the exhibit bears directly on the issue.

Court: Objection overruled. The exhibit is received.

Plaintiff's Attorney: May I hand the exhibit to the jury, your honor?

Court: Permission granted.

Rule Reference

Federal Evidence Rule 403. Exclusion of Relevant Evidence on Grounds of Prejudice, Confusion, or Waste of Time. Although relevant, evidence may be excluded if its probative value is substantially outweighed by the danger of unfair prejudice, confusion of the issues, or misleading the jury, or by considerations of undue delay, waste of time, or needless presentation of cumulative evidence.

Cases and Authorities

See *American Wrecking Corp. v. Secretary of Labor*, 351 F.3d 1254, 1262 (D.C. Cir. 2003)(holding reliance on photograph as accurate depiction of accident scene appropriate where demolition supervisor with knowledge testified photograph reflected fair representation of site prior to accident). Elements of proof, see *United States v. Patterson*, 277 F.3d 709, 713 (4th Cir. 2002)(discussing foundation requirements for photographs).

Comment

The principle underlying the admission of photographs allows their introduction as exhibits when they have been authenticated by the operator of the camera, or by some other witness who can testify from personal knowledge as to the accuracy of the representation.

Reference on photographs, see 9 Am. Jur. Proof of Facts 147; 3 Am Jur Trials 1, Preparing and using photographs in civil cases. Motion pictures, see 8 Am. Jur. Proof of Facts 153. Day in the life videotapes, see 38 Am. Jur. Trials 261. Foundation for admission of videotape evidence generally, see 16 Am. Jur. Proof of Facts 3d 493.

When photographs are dramatic or gory, potent objections to them are often mounted under Federal Evidence Rule 403. However, courts have been liberal in the admission of gruesome photographs. See *United States v. Bowers*, 660 F.2d 527, 529–30 (5th Cir. 1981); *Maxwell v. State*, 250 Ga.App. 628, 552 S.E.2d 870 (2001)(photos of severely injured victim of assault, however gruesome, are not objectionable merely because there is other evidence of severity of victim's injuries); *Washburn v. Beatt Equipment Co.*, 120 Wash.2d 246, 840 P.2d 860 (1992). There are, of course, decisions on the other side. In one case, the defendant moved in limine to exclude a photo of an injured leg, which looked like "hamburger." Under Rule 403, the photos were deemed more prejudicial than probative. The photos depicted "blood and gore which is highly prejudicial to the defendant in this case," held the North Dakota Supreme Court. Hamilton v. Oppen, 2002 ND 185, 653 N.W.2d 678 (2002).

Present Sense Impression

Elements

Sometimes two people witness a dramatic event, and one remarks about it to the other. The latter does not appear at trial when the event is litigated, but the former person does, and he seeks to testify to the other person's remark. To prove it up, counsel should follow these elements: 1) the trial witness reports the statement of another, frequently when both the witness and the declarant have observed the same event; 2) the declarant made his statement describing the event while he was a witness to its occurrence, or immediately thereafter; 3) the declarant had personal knowledge of the events which he described.

Direct Examination

Q. (by plaintiff's attorney) Mr. Gardner, did you see some skid marks at the scene?

A. I sure did. Back from the defendant's car about 80 or 90 feet, up to where the two cars were mashed together.

Q. Had you seen one of the two cars that were mashed together at some time earlier that day?

A. Yes. This was about 3 miles before the wreck, travelling on Oak Street. A car came around me, a Monte Carlo. Later, when I came up to the scene of the crash. I could see it was the same car that had passed me earlier.

Q. Did anyone say anything when the Monte Carlo passed you before the wreck?

A. Yes. My friend Shalimar was riding with me. She dances at the club where I tend bar. We were on our way home. She was in the front passenger's seat, I was driving. When the Monte Carlo went around, she said "Look at him. If that guy keeps up that speed, we will find him in a ditch up the road somewhere." Sure enough, a couple of minutes later we come on this wreck, and there he is.

Objection by Defense: Object, move to strike.

Plaintiff's Attorney: Present sense impression, your honor. Although the woman will not be testifying here, the woman's statement to this witness stands as a hearsay exception.

Court: Objection overruled, and motion denied. The evidence will stand.

Rule Reference

Federal Evidence Rule 803(1) provides that a statement describing or explaining an event or condition made while the declarant was perceiving the event or condition, or immediately thereafter is not excluded by the hearsay rule, even though the declarant is available as a witness.

Cases and Authorities

The facts of the foregoing Q. and A. are close to the facts of *Houston Oxygen Co. v. Davis*, 139 Tex. 1, 161 S.W.2d 474, 476–77 (1942). Courts continue to litigate what is and what is not a present sense impression. See *United States v. Ruiz*, 249 F.3d 643 (7th Cir. 2001)(police officer heard declarant describe drug deal over walkie-talkie); *Jonas v. Isuzu Motors Ltd.*, 210 F.Supp.2d 1373, 1378–79 (M.D. Ga. 2002) (holding driver's out-of-court statement, which was heard by three eyewitness, that he fell asleep at wheel, killed his father and wanted to die was admissible as present sense impression because it described circumstances of accident in which declarant was just involved). Not admissible, see *1337523 Ontario, Inc. v. Golden State Bancorp, Inc.*, 163 F.Supp.2d 1111, 1120 (N.D. Cal. 2001)(letter written several days after event inadmissible as present sense impression because statement was not made contemporaneously with event).

Comment

The person who made the declaration which is the object of this hearsay exception need not have been excited. The substitute for excitement required in Rule 803(2) declarations, excited utterances, is found in the requirement of substantial contemporaneity of event and statement in this exception.

The witness who reports the declarant's statement can be interrogated regarding the circumstances under which the declarant spoke. There may be occasional cases where the declarant is also a witness at trial and subject to examination.

References, see J. Waltz, *The Present Sense Impression Exception to the Rule Against Hearsay: Origins and Attributes*, 66 Iowa L. Rev. 869 (1981).

In criminal cases, courts may ultimately require compliance with *Crawford v. Washington*, ___ U.S. ___, 124 S.Ct. 1354, 158 L.Ed.2d 177 (2004) when the prosecutor offers a present sense declaration by an out-of-court declarant. The law on this point is evolving. Raising the issue of whether present sense impressions are subject to *Crawford*, see *Ko v. New York*, 2004 WL 595231 (2004). More on *Crawford* see the entry for *Declarations Against Interest in this text*.

Prior Consistent Statements

Elements

Prior consistent statements are valuable tools for supporting a witness, particularly on redirect examination, after he has been vigorously attacked. These are the elements: 1) in advance of the trial the witness who is on the stand authored a prior statement; 2) it is consistent with and corroborates what he said on direct examination; 3) after the witness' direct, he was attacked by a slashing cross-examination which expressly or impliedly accused him of falsifying his story.

Redirect Examination

Q. Mr. Witness, you said on direct examination that you saw the color of the light for my driver?

A. Yes. It was green. The plaintiff had the green light.

Q. On cross-examination the defense accused you of fabricating that fact. Did you do so?

A. No. Absolutely not.

Q. Prior to today, have you ever recounted what you saw at the accident scene?

A. Yes. The day after the wreck I told your investigator what I saw, and I signed a statement about it.

Q. Where did this happen?

A. In my home. She came to my house.

Q. I hand you now what has been marked Plaintiff's Exhibit 9 for identification and ask if you can identify it?

A. Yes, this is the statement I signed last July 9, the day after the accident.

Q. As you look it over, is it a true and accurate statement of the facts?

A. Yes.

Q. Whose signature appears at the bottom of the page on this single page statement?

A. Mine.

Q. Did you freely and voluntarily sign it?

A. Yes.

Plaintiff's Attorney: We offer Plaintiff's Exhibit 9 into evidence, and request permission for the witness to read a relevant paragraph.

Court: The exhibit is received and you may proceed.

Q. Mr. Witness, will you please read the second paragraph?

A. Yes. It says "I saw the whole thing. The day was bright and sunny, and it was about 3 p.m. in the afternoon. The light turned green for the silver Honda, and when that car went into the intersection, the B and L Trucking Company truck roared through a red light and hit the Honda broadside."

Rule Reference

Federal Evidence Rule 801(d)(1)(B) provides a statement is not hearsay if it is "consistent with the declarant's testimony and is offered to rebut an express or implied charge against the declarant of recent fabrication or improper influence or motive."

Cases and Authorities

A leading discussion on this subject is contained in *Tome v. United States*, 513 U.S. 150, 115 S.Ct. 696, 130 L.Ed.2d 574

(1995), which authorizes admission of supportive consistent statements. However, the witness' earlier statement must have been made prior to the onset of any bias or improper influence which was allegedly brought to bear on the witness. Numerous cases allow the sort of bolstering Q. and A. illustrated in this section of the text after a cross-examiner suggests the witness fabricated his story. See *United States v. Ruiz*, 249 F.3d 643 (7th Cir. 2001); *United States v. Stoecker*, 215 F.3d 788 (7th Cir. 2000).

A few words of caution are appropriate. Not every impeachment of a witness will permit rehabilitation by prior consistent statements (must be claim of fabrication or improper motive by the cross-examiner). In addition, introduction of prior consistent statements to support the witness *before* impeachment of the witness can constitute reversible error.

Comment

Prior statements can be supportive. Where they back up the story given by the witness on direct, they help to persuade the trier of fact that the witness has consistently told the truth. What is required is that the witness be attacked, on cross-examination or otherwise, with a direct or implied claim of fabrication. Then the witness can be sustained by a prior statement. Thus, this form of proof is often made on redirect examination, after a slashing attack is made on the witness on cross.

Proof of Facts reference, see 21 Am. Jur. Proof of Facts 2d 101, at §§ 9.5–11.

Prior Convictions

Elements

The elements of prior conviction proof are: 1) a witness has been convicted of a crime amounting to a felony, and, in the case of the accused, the probative worth of the conviction exceeds the prejudicial effect of its exposure; or 2) a witness other than the accused has a felony conviction on his record, the introduction of which would not be unduly prejudicial; or 3) the witness has been convicted of a crime, either felony or misdemeanor, which involved dishonesty or false statement; 4) as to dishonesty and false statement crimes (Rule 609(a)(2)), proposed introduction does not trigger the discretionary judgment element involved with felonies generally and described in Rule 609(a)(1); 5) convictions over ten years old (computation of time described hereafter) are generally inadmissible and will be admitted only rarely and under exceptional circumstances in the interests of justice. (See Rule 609(b)).

Cross-Examination

Q. Mr. Witness, isn't it a fact that you were convicted of assault with a dangerous weapon in state court, and sentenced to a 2 year suspended sentence in 1990?

Objection by opponent: Improper impeachment. Cannot impeach a party in a civil case with a crime which does not involve dishonesty or false statement. Move to strike.

Response: Federal Evidence Rule 609 allows this evidence, your honor.

Court: Overruled.

Cross-examiner: Answer the question, please. Were you convicted?

A. Yes, it happened in the Red Owl Tavern.

Rule Reference

Federal Evidence Rule 609(a). Impeachment by Evidence of Conviction of Crime.

(a) General rule. For the purpose of attacking the credibility of a witness,

(1) evidence that a witness other than an accused has been convicted of a crime shall be admitted, subject to Rule 403, if the crime was punishable by death or imprisonment in excess of one year under the law under which the witness was convicted, and evidence that an accused has been convicted of such a crime shall be admitted if the court determines that the probative value of admitting this evidence outweighs its prejudicial effect to the accused; and

(2) evidence that any witness has been convicted of a crime shall be admitted if it involved dishonesty or false statement, regardless of the punishment.

Cases and Authorities

See *United States v. Johnson*, 302 F.3d 139, 152–53 (3d Cir. 2002)(holding impeachment of defense witness with evidence of prior felony convictions admissible, and stating that introduction of witness's prior conviction did not inflict "unfair prejudice beyond that which ordinarily accompanies evidence introduced pursuant to Rule 609(a)(1)"); *United States v. Howell*, 285 F.3d 1263, 1270 (10th Cir. 2002)(failure of district court to conduct Federal Rule of Evidence 403 balancing test in determining admission of witnesses' felony convictions was abuse of discretion); *United States v. Foster*, 227 F.3d 1096, 1100 (9th Cir. 2000)(receipt of stolen property is not per se crime of dishonesty for purposes of impeachment rule).

Comments

Prior convictions are commonly proved through testimony or by a written record. By the phrase "dishonesty and false statement" the drafters of Rule 609 envisioned such crimes as perjury, false statement, criminal fraud, embezzlement, false pretenses, or any other offense in the nature of *crimen falsi*. Ordinance violations have been ruled in a number of jurisdictions to be outside the rule allowing impeachment by prior conviction of crime.

When inquiry about a felony or other crime is made, the examiner is usually barred from dredging up aggravating details; and is limited to the name of the crime, the date the offense, and the disposition of the matter. *Hernandez v. Cepeda*, 860 F.2d 260, 264 (7th Cir. 1988). Some states are more limited. A few courts disallow prior conviction impeachment. Others restrict the examiner to the question of whether the witness has been previously convicted of a felony, without naming it, or a crime involving dishonesty. See *Jackson v. State*, 570 So.2d 1388 (Fla. 1st DCA 1990).

A good-faith basis is usually required for inquiry about prior crimes.

Remote convictions are generally barred by the rule which provides that old convictions are not admissible if more than ten years has elapsed since the date of the conviction or the release of the witness form confinement, *whichever event is later*. An attorney seeking to circumvent this rule of remoteness must supply advance written notice to the adversary.

Finally, a 1990 amendment to Rule 609 makes clear that witnesses may reveal on Direct Examination their convictions to "remove the sting" of the impeachment. There is case authority that when this is done accurately on direct, further cross-examination on the point is foreclosed. *See, e.g., Nicholas v. State*, 49 Wis.2d 683, 183 N.W.2d 11, at 15–16 (Wis. 1971). See also *United States v. Freeman*, 302 F.2d 347, 350 (2d Cir. 1962); *Cummings v. State*, 412 So.2d 436 (Fla. Dist.

Ct. App. 4th Dist. 1982). However, this "anticipation" technique may have one downside. If defense counsel filed a motion in limine attempting to block a prior conviction and lost, she may wish to appeal that evidentiary decision, in the event the accused loses at trial. Under a 2000 United States Supreme Court decision, that appeal may be difficult if defense counsel herself brought out the prior on direct examination. See *Ohler v. United States*, 529 U.S. 753, 760, 120 S.Ct. 1851, 1855, 146 L.Ed.2d 826 (2000)(a defendant who preemptively introduces evidence of a prior conviction on direct examination may not appeal his claim that the admission of such evidence was error).

Proof of Facts reference, see 36 Am. Jur. Proof of Facts 2d 747. For a critical look at Rule 609, see R. Dodson, *What Went Wrong with Federal Rule of Evidence 609: A Hard Look at How Jurors Really Misuse Prior conviction Evidence,* 48 Drake L. Rev. 1 (1999).

Prior Impeaching Statements

Elements

An effective attack may be made on an opposing witness by using his prior inconsistent statements against him. The attacking lawyer needs to show: 1) the trial witness authored a prior oral or written statement; 2) the statement contradicts the witness' trial testimony; 3) the witness is confronted with the statement by the examiner; 4) when doing so, the examiner identifies the time and place of making the statement and the individual to whom made; 5) if the cross-examiner seeks to prove up an inconsistent written statement by calling an extrinsic witness to authenticate it, it must be displayed to the impeached witness for his inspection.

Cross-Examination

Q. You said on Direct Examination that the Smith car was traveling "real fast, about 40 m.p.h." Is that correct?

A. Correct, yes.

Q. Have you ever stated your observation of the speed to be a different figure, very much slower?

A. Never.

Q. Do you remember December 20, the afternoon of the day after the accident, that a man came to your house?

A. Could be, I'm not certain.

Q. Isn't that when you met Mr. Floyd Walker, an independent investigator who met with you in your kitchen that day?

A. I guess maybe I did. I sort of remember now.

Counsel: Please mark this statement for identification. **(Clerk does so)** Mr. Witness, I hand you what the clerk has marked defendant's exhibit 1 for identification and direct your attention to the bottom of page one, the only page in the exhibit. Isn't that your signature?

A. It looks like it. Yes, it is.

Q. And didn't you sign this statement, consisting of one page?

A. I guess I did, yes.

Q. And in this statement, referring specifically to lines 6 through 8, you said: "I saw the whole thing. The green car, which I now know was driven by Mr. Smith, was moving from west to east, traveling deliberately and at a speed of about 20 m.p.h."

A. Yes.

Q. When were the details of this incident fresher in your mind, Mr. Clinton. At the time of this statement or now, a year after the accident?

A. I'm not sure.

Q. Let me rephrase. As to the words about the speed of the Smith car, were they given for purposes of this written statement at a time closer to the accident than the story you gave today on Direct Examination?

A. The statement was closer in time to the accident, of course.

Counsel: That's all.

Rule Reference

Federal Evidence Rule 613. Prior statements of witnesses.

(a) Examining witness concerning prior statement. In examining a witness concerning a prior statement made by the

witness, whether written or not, the statement need not be shown nor its contents disclosed to the witness at that time, but on request the same shall be shown or disclosed to opposing counsel.

(b) Extrinsic evidence of prior inconsistent statement of witness. Extrinsic evidence of a prior inconsistent statement by opportunity to interrogate the witness thereon, or the interests of justice otherwise require. This provision does not apply to admissions of a party-opponent as defined in rule 801(d)(2).

Cases and Authorities

Prior statements authored by an opposing witness may be used to confront her at trial. These prior declarations may be drawn from the witness' depositions, written statements, oral conversations or business files. *Travelers Ins. Co. v. Smith,* 338 Ark. 81, 991 S.W.2d 591 (1999). Impeachment can also come from the witness' prior inconsistent acts. *Brandt v. Vulcan, Inc.,* 30 F.3d 752 (7th Cir. 1994). In order to allow prior inconsistent statement impeachment, the trial judge must decide if the prior declaration of the witness is truly inconsistent with his trial testimony. *Lentomyynti Oy v. Medivac, Inc.,* 997 F.2d 364, 373 (7th Cir. 1993); *United States v. Bonnett,* 877 F.2d 1450, 1463 (10th Cir. 1989).

In order to introduce evidence of a prior statement during a party's case, the party must first have confronted the witness who is attacked by the statement and must have given him a chance to explain it. See *United States v. Schnapp,* 322 F.3d 564, 571–72 (8th Cir. 2003)(holding exclusion of defendant's impeachment testimony regarding alleged prior inconsistent statements of government witness was warranted where defense counsel failed to ask witness to explain or deny alleged prior statements while witness was on stand during government's case-in-chief).

Comment

The cross-examination Q. and A. from the above transcript reflects an impeachment using a prior writing. Rule 613 controls this example. The impeachment process is complete in the foregoing transcript. Having validated the statement, the view of most courts is that the witness has been damaged enough and the full introduction of the writing into evidence would accomplish little. *BankAtlantic v. Blythe Eastman Paine Webber, Inc.,* 955 F.2d 1467, 1476 (11th Cir. 1992). Of course, where the witness denies making the statement, an authenticating witness (investigator Walker) may be called later by the defense during its case and the statement itself offered.

Statements used to impeach a witness are usually treated as credibility evidence, and not substantive proof. A jury instruction to this effect is appropriate. *United States v. Larry Reed & Sons Partnership,* 280 F.3d 1212, 1215 (8th Cir. 2002)(failure to give jury limiting instruction about purpose of prior statement testimony was error, but in the absence of a trial objection was not plain error); *United States v. Gochis,* 169 F.Supp.2d 918, 920 (N.D. Ill. 2001)(prior inconsistent statements properly admitted and proper limiting instruction given).

While usually received as credibility evidence only, there is one scenario where the impeaching document is viewed as substantive proof. It may be used as substantive evidence if the declarant is subject to cross-examination at the current trial, and the prior inconsistent statement was given under oath at an earlier trial, hearing or similar proceeding. Rule 801(d)(1)(A), Federal Rules of Evidence (prior inconsistent statements which were given *under oath* treated as substantive evidence).

Privileges

Elements

The basic elements for establishing a privilege include the following factors: 1) party asserting confidentiality is the holder of a privilege; 2) communication was with or by a person who was a client, patient, or otherwise sought professional help; 3) statements were made in the course of a professional relationship; 4) communication was intended to be confidential; 5) the relationship is recognized as a privileged one under applicable federal or state law.

Cross-Examination

In the following case, the plaintiff's attorney was required to call an investigator from his office to authenticate a signed statement of another witness, which statement the investigator had taken. The investigator is cross-examined.

Q. **(by defense)** You are an investigator in the Herndon law offices?

A. Yes.

Q. What did the plaintiff in this case, a client of your office, tell you about his gambling problems which preceded the incident which caused this case to come to court?

Objection by proponent of witness: Objection, beyond the scope of the direct and privileged. The witness did not touch upon any conversations with the plaintiff during her direct. Could I have a brief voir dire to establish privilege, your honor?

Court: Permission granted.

Q. (by plaintiff's attorney) During the conversation with the plaintiff which opposing counsel referred to, was anyone else present?

A. No. We talked in the law firm conference room, and the doors were shut and we were alone.

Q. Did the plaintiff tell you why he came to the office?

A. He said he came to see Mr. Herndon about his case, and when Mr. Herndon was not there, he talked to me with information for Mr. Herndon.

Proponent of witness, Plaintiff's Attorney: We object to any further testimony about this conversation.

Court: Objection sustained. A privileged communication has been established.

Rule Reference

Federal Evidence Rule 501. General Rule. Except as otherwise required by the Constitution of the United States or provided by Act of Congress or in rules prescribed by the Supreme Court pursuant to statutory authority, the privilege of a witness, person, government, State, or political subdivision thereof shall be governed by the principles of the common law as they may be interpreted by the courts of the United States in the light of reason and experience. However, in civil actions and proceedings, with respect to an element of a claim or defense as to which State law supplies the rule of decision, the privilege of a witness, person, government, State, or political subdivision thereof shall be determined in accordance with State law.

Cases and Authorities

The *Attorney-Client Privilege* rests upon the need for confidential legal advice and is discussed in *Upjohn Co. v. United States*, 449 U.S. 383, 101 S.Ct. 677, 66 L.Ed.2d 584

(1981)(corporate attorney-client privilege) and *United States v. Zolin*, 491 U.S. 554, 109 S.Ct. 2619, 105 L.Ed.2d 469 (1989)(crime or fraud exception to privilege). The *Marital Privilege* protects conversations between spouses in order to foster marital harmony, and is discussed in cases like *Trammel v. United States*, 445 U.S. 40, 100 S.Ct. 906, 63 L.Ed.2d 186 (1980) and *United States v. Singleton*, 260 F.3d 1295 (11th Cir. 2001)(discussing marital privilege). The *Psychotherapist-Patient Privilege* provides confidentiality for patients seeking and receiving mental health advice, and is discussed in *Jaffee v. Redmond*, 518 U.S. 1, 116 S.Ct. 1923, 135 L.Ed.2d 337 (1996)(covers conversations by patients or clients with licensed psychiatrists, psychologists and social workers). The *Work Product Privilege* protects a lawyer's memoranda, statements and mental impressions and is discussed in *Hickman v. Taylor*, 329 U.S. 495, 67 S.Ct. 385, 91 L.Ed. 451 (1947) and *Pamida Inc. v. E.S. Originals, Inc.*, 281 F.3d 726, 731–32 (8th Cir. 2002)(waiver of work product privilege). Reporters and writers can often claim a privilege to protect the confidentiality of their sources under a *Newsgatherer's Privilege*, discussed in cases like *Herbert v. Lando*, 441 U.S. 153, 99 S.Ct. 1635, 60 L.Ed.2d 115 (1979) and *United States v. Hively,* 202 F.Supp.2d 886, 892–93 (E.D. Ark. 2002)(discussing federal court's authorization under Fed. R. Evid. 501 to define new privileges by interpreting common-law principles in light of reason and experience, and declining to recognize a common-law reporters' privilege where newspaper reporter's proposed testimony would not impact confidentiality nor intrude into any relationship of trust). There are other privileges as well, including those covering clergy-communicant conversations, a privilege for government informers, military and state secrets, account-client disclosures, and others.

Comments

Unless waived, private communications with a lawyer relating to legal advice are privileged. So are statements to a lawyer's employee, made to assist in preparing the client's case and intended for communication to the lawyer.

Numerous other privileges are commonly available, and some of these include privileges for purposes of medical treatment, trade secrets, and a banker-depositor privilege in some locations. The Fifth Amendment privilege against self-incrimination can be asserted in a proper context, and some jurisdictions recognize protection for environmental self-audits.

Jurisdictional variations exist, and a number of privileges are listed in R. Carlson, Successful Techniques for Civil Trials 2d §§ 8:15–8:24 (1992). Proof of Facts reference, see 45 Am. Jur. Proof of Facts 2d 595, at § 2 (physician-patient privilege). Comprehensive treatment of the law of privilege in American courts, see E. Imwinkelried, The New Wigmore; A Treatise on Evidence: Evidentiary Privileges (2002).

Public Records

Elements

A public document often supplies a needed element of a party's proof. It is properly introduced when: 1) a record is kept by a public office or agency, pursuant to law; 2) a certified copy is presented in court, or a witness may testify that a copy is correct after comparing it with the original.

Direct Examination

Plaintiff's Attorney: Doctor, were you in the emergency room when the passenger in the plaintiff's car died?

A. Yes.

Q. Do you have the copy of the death certificate with you for the passenger who died?

A. Yes, I brought it along at your request.

Q. (certificate is marked as plaintiff's exhibit 3) Has the document which has been marked plaintiff's exhibit 3 been certified?

A. Yes. It bears the official certification of the office of the county medical examiner.

Q. Does it show the cause of death?

A. Yes. The medical examiner apparently spoke briefly to this passenger, who then lapsed into a coma and died. After the autopsy, the medical examiner filled out the death certificate and recorded the following: The passenger died as a result of massive head injuries incurred in an automobile accident. He expired after suffering a cerebral hemorrhage; death occurred about 20 minutes after his arrival at the hospital.

Plaintiff's Attorney: We offer plaintiff's exhibit 3 into evidence.

Defense Attorney: Objection. Move to strike, your honor. We stipulate that the death certificate is an official document properly authenticated, but object on the ground of hearsay.

Court: Overruled.

Rule Reference

Federal Evidence Rule 803. The following are not excluded by the hearsay rule, even though the declarant is available as a witness.

. . .

(8) Public records and reports. Records, reports, statements, or data compilations, in any form, of public offices or agencies, setting forth (A) the activities of the office or agency, or (B) matters observed pursuant to duty imposed by law as to which matters there was a duty to report, excluding, however, in criminal cases matters observed by police officers and other law enforcement personnel, or (C) in civil actions and proceedings and against the government in criminal cases, factual findings resulting from an investigation made pursuant to authority granted by law, unless the sources of information or other circumstances indicate lack of trustworthiness.

Cases and Authorities

See *United States v. McIntosh*, 200 F.3d 1168, 1169 (8th Cir. 2000)(certified court documents admitted as public records); *Union Pac. R.R. Co. v. Kirby Inland Marine, Inc. of Mississippi*, 296 F.3d 671, 679 (8th Cir. 2002)(finding Coast Guard order admissible under hearsay exception for public records and reports since Coast Guard investigation mandated by Truman–Hobbs Act, Coast Guard reliance on hearsay evidence to reach conclusions did not mean report preparation was untrustworthy). A significant issue sometimes develops over opinions in public records, as discussed in *Beech Aircraft Corp. v. Rainey*, 488 U.S. 153, 109 S.Ct. 439, 102 L.Ed.2d 445 (1988). One of the chief arenas for dispute is whether conclusions drawn from factual findings developed by an administrative agency will be admitted. Admitting such evidence, see *United States v. Midwest Fireworks Manufacturing Co.*, 248 F.3d 563, 566 (6th Cir. 2001)(presumption of admissibility); *Zeus Enterprises, Inc. v. Alphin Aircraft, Inc.*, 190 F.3d 238, 241 (4th Cir. 1999)(administrative law judge for National Transportation Safety Board found aircraft not "airworthy"; decision of ALJ was admissible in aircraft owner's breach of contract action against a company). Excluding, see *Lathem v. Department of Children and Youth Services*, 172 F.3d 786, 791–2 (11th Cir. 1999)(noting distinction between jury and bench trials).

Legal conclusions in public documents (i.e., "this was negligence" or "this was malpractice") are often excluded. See, e.g., *Brom v. Bozell, Jacobs, Kenyon & Eckhardt, Inc.*, 867 F.Supp. 686 (N.D. Ill. 1994)(presenting administrative agency's conclusion on a charge of discrimination would be "tantamount to saying this has already been decided and here is the decision").

Burden of proof when offering a public document, the party opposing admission of a public record under the public records exception has the burden of establishing record's unreliability, see *Reynolds v. Green*, 184 F.3d 589, 596 (6th Cir. 1999)(records presumed to be trustworthy).

Comment

A copy of a public record required by law to be kept by a federal, state, city or county office is competent evidence when the copy is duly certified by the director or a qualified deputy of the public office. An example is a weather report certified by the chief meteorologist in charge of a regional weather station. The proffer might sound something like this:

Counsel: **(to court reporter)** Please mark this for identification.

(To court): If the court please, at this time I offer what has been marked plaintiff's exhibit 8 for identification, which is a certified copy of the weather report for the month of July, 1999, from the United States weather station nearest in point of distance to the scene of the occurrence, in evidence as plaintiff's exhibit 8.

Court: It will be received.

Note that the form of the certification appearing as part of a public record may be prescribed by federal statute where the report comes from a U.S. government agency, or state statute in other cases. Weather reports, see 5 Am. Jur. Proof of Facts 3d 191.

Qualifications of Expert

Elements

In order to provide the trier of fact with technical or specialized information, an expert witness must be called and qualified. Satisfying the court that there is a need for expert testimony and that the person called to testify can supply it requires these steps: 1) a witness is summoned to testify on a specialized topic; 2) knowledge, experience or education qualifies the witness as an expert on the topic; 3) the expert's testimony and opinions will assist the trier of fact; 4) the topic is one beyond the ken of ordinary lay persons.

Direct Examination

Q. (by plaintiff's attorney in a products liability case) Will you state your name, please?

A. Fairchild Neverrer.

Q. Where do you live?

A. 1107 Flotsom Lane, Gotham City.

Q. What is your business or occupation?

A. Automotive Design Engineer.

Q. Please state your educational background.

A. After receiving my bachelors degree in Engineering from Washington University in St. Louis, I took my masters in Engineering from the Massachusetts Institute of Technology. In 2002 I completed my education with a Ph.D. in Engineering from the California Institute of Technology.

Q. During that educational training have you had the opportunity to study stress factors related to such metals as are used in the manufacture of automobiles?

A. Yes. An important part of my educational component consisted of such metals research.

Q. Have you prepared or published research on the subject?

A. Yes, I have published two articles in professional journals on this subject. My latest, "Stress and Fatigue in the Construction of Auto Frames" appeared in the January 2005 issue of "Auto Design Engineer."

Q. Does your current experience include inspecting and testing various features of motor vehicles?

A. Yes. I am the Associate Dean of the Mechanical Engineering Department here at Gotham College in the city. The portions of the curriculum for which I have responsibility include the automobile design offerings. In connection with those courses, I do a great deal of study and testing of passenger motor vehicles, both domestic and foreign.

Q. Do you inspect and test automobile fuel systems?

A. Yes, I do.

Q. In addition to your duties connected with your profession have you engaged in other study of the fuel systems of automobiles?

A. Yes, I am a consultant to the National Safety Council.

Specifically, my consultantship is in the field of fuel system and exhaust system design.

Q. Doctor, over the years how many fuel systems have you studied?

A. Systems, 30 or 40, at least. In terms of actual cars which I have inspected, that would number over 1,000.

Q. Have you studied the cause and effect of auto accidents on motor vehicle fuel systems?

A. Yes.

Q. What are your professional society memberships?

A. American Society of Mechanical Engineers, State Society of Mechanical Engineers, American Society of Automotive Engineers.

Q. Have you testified in court cases before?

A. Yes.

Q. About how many times?

A. 12 times.

Q. And have you always testified for the plaintiff, Doctor Neverrer?

A. No. You asked me to check my records and I have testified for auto companies on nine of the twelve occasions.

(at this point, the expert's testimony turns to the merits of the case)

Rule Reference

Federal Evidence Rule 702. Testimony by Experts. If scientific, technical, or other specialized knowledge will assist the trier of fact to understand the evidence or to determine a fact in issue, a witness qualified as an expert by knowledge, skill, experience, training, or education, may testify thereto in the form of an opinion or otherwise, if (1) the testimony is based upon sufficient facts or data, (2) the testimony is the product of reliable principles and methods, and (3) the witness has applied the principles and methods reliably to the facts of the case.

Cases and Authorities

Cases in which experts were deemed to be qualified include *United States v. McPhilomy*, 270 F.3d 1302, 1312–13 (10th

Cir. 2001)(geologist qualified by education and experience to testify as expert on the value of stone) and *Groobert v. President & Dirs. of Georgetown Coll.*, 219 F.Supp.2d 1, 7–11 (D.D.C. 2002) (determining personal experience proper method for assessing reliability of expert testimony regarding future earnings of deceased stock photographer in absence of reports or studies on income of stock photographers, and concluding that testimony of photographic production company owner with twelve years exclusive work in stock photography was reliable and admissible).

Comment

The foregoing trial proof contained in the Q. and A. is drawn from an exploding gas tank litigation. The car burst into flames and the plaintiff was burned. Other particulars of the expert's testimony, including his opinion that a different fuel system design would have prevented the calamity, appear in R. Carlson, Successful Techniques for Civil Trials 2d § 4:29 (1992). Advice is also contained there for the lawyer who faces the following challenge: The opponent who offers to stipulate to the expert's qualifications when you want to bring them out. Carlson, supra at § 4:23. Questions for qualifying medical experts, see 33 Am. Jur. Proof of Facts 2d 179.

Experts may be qualified by experience or education or both. Experts like physicians and engineers will be asked about academic degrees, specialized training, when the witness was licensed (where licensing is a feature of the profession), number of years of experience, past contact with the particular problem at issue in the case, lectures or articles in the field by the expert, membership in professional associations, and prior experience as an expert witness on the topic involved in the case. Whether each of these topics will be touched upon in any given situation depends upon the expert's particular background and the strategy involved in the case.

Reconstruction of Accidents

Elements

It can be valuable to call an expert to provide speed or point-of-impact estimates in a car crash case. The following elements need to be shown when the person called to supply expert opinions takes the stand: 1) the expert is qualified as an expert in the dynamics of vehicle accidents; 2) as a basis for his opinion, the expert factors into his decision the operative data in the specific case, including physical damage and skid marks as illustrated in the following Q. and A. proof; 3) the witness gives an opinion regarding the speed of a vehicle or vehicles involved in an accident, or the place of impact between vehicles, or the path which cars took immediately prior to the crash, or other relevant matters.

Direct Examination

Q. Ms. Expert, you have previously identified in your testimony the factors you considered in arriving at your conclusions, including the length and location of the skid marks laid down by both vehicles, location of debris including dirt, chrome and glass, physical damage to the surrounding area, weather conditions on the day of the wreck, extent of grade and nature of the road surface and the location and extent of damage to both vehicles. Based on these things, do you have an opinion as to the original point of impact between these two vehicles?

A. Yes.

Q. Will you please give us your opinion?

A. In my opinion, the original point of contact was about 8
feet south of the center line, in the Smyth car's lane of
travel. The Wheeler vehicle came across the middle of the
roadway and collided head-on with the Smyth car, in my
view, with primary damage to the left front and driver's
side of the Smyth automobile.

Rule Reference

Federal Evidence Rule 702. Testimony by Experts. If scientific, technical, or other specialized knowledge will assist the
trier of fact to understand the evidence or to determine a fact
in issue, a witness qualified as an expert by knowledge, skill,
experience, training, or education, may testify thereto in the
form of an opinion or otherwise, if (1) the testimony is based
upon sufficient facts or data, (2) the testimony is the product
of reliable principles and methods, and (3) the witness has
applied the principles and methods reliably to the facts of the
case.

Cases and Authorities

Vehicle accidents are the sort of mishap usually testified
about when an accident reconstructionist takes the stand. See
Jodoin v. Toyota Motor Corp., Inc., 284 F.3d 272 (1st Cir.
2002) (plaintiff's expert tested truck for rollover propensity;
admissibility of reconstructive evidence will be approved when
test conditions are substantially similar to facts of original
accident); *Miles v. General Motors Corp.*, 262 F.3d 720, 724
(8th Cir. 2001) (affirmed admission of accident reconstruction
testimony to show how motorcyclist received injuries in accident). Occasionally, however, the expert is called upon to
perform other functions. See *Stotts v. Heckler & Koch, Inc.*,
299 F.Supp.2d 814 (W.D. Tenn. 2004)(holding forensic pathologist who was experienced in determining cause of death could
provide expert opinion testimony regarding bullet trajectory

through skull and probability of suicide or homicide; however, due to lack of accident reconstruction training, his opinion regarding location of gun when fired was not based on reliable methodology but assumed facts and speculation, and opinion was of no assistance to trier of fact).

Comment

An officer, or other expert, if shown to be qualified, may properly base an estimate as to speed of the vehicles at the time of the collision upon skid marks, but frequently cannot do so solely upon physical impact damage to the automobiles. Some courts which allow speed estimates do not permit point of impact or path of vehicle testimony; others allow these opinions.

A mechanical engineer was permitted to offer an opinion on how an accident occurred in *Bornn v. Madagan*, 414 N.W.2d 646 (Iowa Ct. App. 1987). Qualifications of expert, see *Loseke v. Mables*, 217 Ill.App.3d 521, 160 Ill.Dec. 471, 577 N.E.2d 796 (3d Dist. 1991)(investigating officer). Reconstruction of traffic accidents, see 9 Am. Jur. Proof of Facts 3d 115. Speed, see Am. Jur. 11 Proof of Facts 1.

Remedial Measures

Elements

While remedial measures taken by a defendant are regularly excluded, there are important exceptions to the rule of exclusion. Proving up remedial conduct under one of these exceptions requires the proponent of the evidence to show: 1) the opposing party engaged in a subsequent safety measure which is relevant to the case; 2) the offering party establishes the remedial action through a qualified witness, on direct or cross-examination; 3) the testimony is offered for a proper purpose such as proving ownership, control, or feasibility of precautionary measures (if controverted), or impeachment.

Cross Examination

Q. (by plaintiff's attorney in a products liability case) Ms. Wallace, you are the vice-president for automobile design at Marathon Motor Company?

A. Yes.

Q. The Marathon Marauder that was rear ended and exploded in this case, what year was that car?

A. A 2002 Marauder.

Q. You stated on Direct Examination that the gasoline tank was mounted behind the rear axle on that model?

A. That was the only place you could put it. As I stated, it wasn't possible to move it forward on that car.

Q. Where did you place the tank on the 2003 models, the next model year?

Objection by Defense: Remedial measures violation, your honor.

Response by Plaintiff: Feasibility exception, your honor.

Court: Overruled.

Q. (by plaintiff's attorney) Will you please address the design of the fuel system on the 2003 cars?

A. We moved to a saddle type tank and put it on top of the axle.

Q. The dimensions on the rear of the 2003 car exactly matched those on the 2002 Marauder, didn't they?

A. Yes.

Q. So the tank was installed more toward the middle of the car and further away from rear end impacts on later models?

A. Correct.

Rule Reference

Federal Rule of Evidence 407. Subsequent Remedial Measures. When, after an event, measures are taken which, if taken previously, would make the event less likely to occur, evidence of the subsequent measures is not admissible to prove negligence, culpable conduct, a defect in a product, a defect in a product's design, or a need for a warning or instruction. This rule does not require the exclusion of evidence of subsequent measures when offered for another purpose, such as proving ownership, control, or feasibility of precautionary measures, if controverted, or impeachment.

Cases and Authorities

On the impeachment exception to the exclusionary rule, see *Stecyk v. Bell Helicopter Textron, Inc.*, 295 F.3d 408 (3d Cir. 2002)(even though evidence of post-incident remedial measure would have served to impeach, court has discretion to exclude as highly prejudicial); *Wood v. Morbark Industries, Inc.*, 70 F.3d 1201 (11th Cir. 1995) (remedial design change after an accident was admissible for impeachment purposes where expert called by company testified original design was the safest possible approach). Feasibility exception, see *Tuer v. McDonald*, 347 Md. 507, 701 A.2d 1101 (1997). Admitting evidence, see *Colegrove v. Cameron Machine Co.*, 172 F.Supp.2d 611, 635 (W.D. Pa. 2001)(photograph showing foot switch with guard on it was admissible subsequent remedial measure where photo was offered to show the position of the foot switch, rather than to show design defect).

On the general rule excluding remedial conduct, see *Stecyk v. Bell Helicopter Textron, Inc.*, supra at 415–16 (noting that Fed. R. Evid. 407 rests on strong public policy of encouraging manufacturers to make safety improvements whether or not they are at fault).

Comment

While generally excluded, subsequent remedial measures are occasionally admissible where offered for reasons other than to prove negligence or culpable conduct, as the foregoing Q. and A. proof illustrates. In addition, remedial measures taken by a party *other* than the defendant are admissible. Thus, where relevant, evidence that a third party has undertaken changes or modifications for safety purposes can be shown. See *Mehojah v. Drummond*, 56 F.3d 1213, 1215 (10th Cir. 1995). Where changes are mandated by the government, they have been held to be admissible. Finally, while safety measures are improper to prove defendant's negligence or culpable conduct, the rule permits admission of this evidence when offered to impeach a party or to prove ownership, control, or feasibility of precautionary measures.

The remedial measures rule has been applied to exclude such evidence in products liability actions. However, a number of state courts have refused to apply the doctrine in products cases. For the division of authorities, see R. Carlson, Successful Techniques for Civil Trials 2d §§ 2:23, 4:29 (1992); 74 ALR 3d 1001.

Scientific Process or Technique

Elements

To establish the reliability of scientific evidence, these are the elements: 1) the expert is qualified in a scientific technique or process; 2) the technique is explained and its reliability established; 3) the technical field which relates most directly to the process is identified; 4) the extent of acceptance by professionals in that field of the process is described; 5) the test or process at issue was correctly carried out in this case; 6) if the technique has been tested, establish the error rate; 7) where the methodology has been published, the fact of publication in a peer-reviewed journal will be relevant.

Direct Examination

Q. (after qualifying expert and presenting preliminary proof) Were sufficient experiments conducted to achieve a DNA match, doctor?

A. Yes.

Q. Did you find a match?

A. Yes. The DNA from the crime scene sample and the known specimen from the accused matched.

A. Can you interpret what that means?

Objection: Improper scientific evidence.

Proponent of witness: Your honor, I will be glad to ask another question to supply additional foundation. Doctor, is DNA testing and interpretation generally accepted by scientists in your field?

A. Yes. There is wide acceptance by pathologists of DNA identification techniques (expert supplies any available particulars).

Q. Will you interpret your results here?

A. Only one person out of every 200,000 will have all the similarities to the crime scene specimen which the accused possesses.

Rule Reference

Federal Evidence Rule 702. Testimony by Experts.

If scientific, technical, or other specialized knowledge will assist the trier of fact to understand the evidence or to determine a fact in issue, a witness qualified as an expert by knowledge, skill, experience, training, or education, may testify thereto in the form of an opinion or otherwise, if (1) the testimony is based upon sufficient facts or data, (2) the testimony is the product of reliable principles and methods, and (3) the witness has applied the principles and methods reliably to the facts of the case.

Cases and Authorities

See *Frye v. United States*, 54 App.D.C. 46, 293 F. 1013 (D.C. Cir. 1923); *Daubert v. Merrell Dow Pharmaceuticals, Inc.*, 509 U.S. 579, 113 S.Ct. 2786, 125 L.Ed.2d 469 (1993); *Kumho Tire Co. v. Carmichael*, 526 U.S. 137, 119 S.Ct. 1167, 143 L.Ed.2d 238 (1999).

The governing legal standards include the *Frye* general acceptance test and the competing standard enunciated in *Daubert* and its progeny, including the Supreme Court's 1999 decision in *Kumho Tire Co. v. Carmichael*. See Imwinkelried and Tobin, Comparative Bullet Lead Analysis (CBLA) Evidence: Valid Inference or Ipse Dixit?, 28 Okla. City. L. Rev. 43, 46 (2003).

Authors Imwinkelried and Tobin sketched the evolution of the law from *Frye* to *Daubert*, and confirmed the presence of the "general acceptance" *Frye* test in many state trials today. In 1923, the Court of Appeals for the District of Columbia handed down its decision in *Frye v. United States*. In *Frye*, the court pronounced that before an expert may base courtroom testimony on a scientific theory, the expert's proponent must lay a foundation establishing that the theory is generally accepted within the relevant scientific circles. At one time, *Frye* was the controlling test in federal court and forty-five of the states.

The Supreme Court in *Daubert v. Merrell Dow Pharmaceuticals, Inc.*, ruled that *Frye* is no longer good federal law. However, the *Daubert* decision was based on statutory construction rather than constitutional analysis. Hence, even in the states with evidence codes patterned after the Federal Rules, the state courts remain free to interpret their statutes differently and to continue to adhere to *Frye*. As of 2004, eighteen states had opted to continue to adhere to *Frye*. Significantly, that number included jurisdictions such as California, Florida, Illinois, New York, Pennsylvania, and Washington. Since these jurisdictions are among the most populous and litigious states, even today *Frye* is the governing law in a significant number of state trials. Imwinkelried and Tobin, supra at 54–55.

While federal courts and some states are controlled by *Daubert*, a few jurisdictions follow standards different from both *Daubert* or *Frye*. See *Williams v. State*, 251 Ga. 749, 312 S.E.2d 40 (1983)(analysis of fibers; to be admissible, process must have reached a scientific state of verifiable certainty).

Cases interpreting and applying *Daubert*, see *Hynes v. Energy West, Inc.*, 211 F.3d 1193, 1205 (10th Cir. 2000)(expert testimony regarding odorization of gas admissible under *Daubert* principles); *United States v. Ewell*, 252 F.Supp.2d 104, 111–15 (D.N.J. 2003)(denying defendant's motion to suppress government's evidence from DNA testing process, where process was capable of verification, subject to peer review and generally accepted, error rate was not significant, and laboratory maintained high standards).

Comment

Novel scientific evidence poses special problems not present when experts from "standard" expert fields (like a mechanical engineer or a psychiatrist) are called to testify. A more particularized foundation is needed. Under the Frye test applied in many state courts, offered proof will be defective if the technical process which is involved is not sufficiently established to have gained general acceptance in the particular field to which it belongs. When the proponent of a new or novel form of scientific proof wishes to offer such evidence, the proponent should qualify the testifying witness as an expert in the process, show that proper test procedures were used, and establish that there is scientific recognition of the process involved in the test. R. Carlson, 3 Criminal Law Advocacy: Trial Proof, ¶ 5.03(2002). Failure to comply with the general acceptance requirement has caused the rejection of new or novel scientific evidence. Polygraph tests as well as other processes have been excluded. Establishing general acceptance for a scientific process, see Am. Jur. 8 Proof of Facts 3d 749, at § 7.

While many state jurisdictions follow the general scientific acceptance standard of *Frye v. United States*, 54 App.D.C. 46, 293 F. 1013, its strictures led some courts to a more liberal rule even before *Daubert*. See *United States v. Downing*, 753 F.2d 1224 (3d Cir. 1985). In 1993 in *Daubert v. Merrell Dow Pharmaceuticals, Inc.*, 509 U.S. 579, 113 S.Ct. 2786, 125 L.Ed.2d 469 (1993) the Supreme Court rejected *Frye* for federal courts in favor of a liberalized standard. After *Daubert*, the Third Circuit identified eight non-exclusive factors to consider in determining whether a particular scientific method is reliable: "(1) whether a method consists of a testable hypothesis; (2) whether the method has been subjected to peer review; (3) the known or potential rate of error; (4) the existence and maintenance of standards controlling the technique's operation; (5) whether the method is generally accepted; (6) the relationship of the technique to methods which have been established to be reliable; (7) the qualifications of the expert witness testifying based on methodology; and (8) the non-judicial uses to which the method has been put." *In re Paoli R.R. Yard PCB Litig.*, 35 F.3d 717, 742 n.8 (3d Cir. 1994).

On the specific problem involved in the trial proof near the start of this section of the text, DNA matching, see 8 Am. Jur. Proof of Facts 3d 749, Foundation for DNA Fingerprint Evidence.

Sequestration Violation

Elements

It is often valuable to demonstrate that a person violated the court's ruling which ordered witnesses to stay out of the courtroom until they testify. The credibility of the witness who violated the order is thereby damaged. These are the elements: 1) the court has ordered that witnesses should be excluded until they testify, so that they cannot hear the testimony of other witnesses; 2) a witness has violated the court's order; 3) the violator is not a party or other person entitled to remain in court under the special exceptions to the general rule of exclusion.

Direct Examination

Q. We next call Einar Strickland (clerk swears witness) Will you state your name?

A. Einar X. Strickland.

Opponent: Excuse me, your honor. May we approach? (At the bench) Could I briefly voir dire this witness in order to make an objection to his testifying here? I will be brief.

Court: Very well.

Q. (by opponent on voir dire) When this trial started yesterday, did you come into the courtroom and listen to the testimony?

A. Yes.

Q. Did Mr. Kurtis, the lawyer who just called you to the stand, tell you to stay out until you testified?

A. Yes. But my brother was scheduled to testify yesterday, which he did, and I didn't want to miss hearing him.

Q. Did you hear a number of witnesses testify?

A. I slipped into the back of the room and didn't disturb anybody. Yes, I heard most of the witnesses who testified yesterday.

Motion by opponent: I move to disqualify this witness for willful violation of the court's ruling which excluded witnesses.

Court: Granted.

Rule Reference

Federal Rule of Evidence 615. Exclusion of Witnesses.

At the request of a party the court shall order witnesses excluded so that they cannot hear the testimony of other witnesses, and it may make the order of its own motion. This rule does not authorize exclusion of (1) a party who is a natural person, or (2) an officer or employee of a party which is not a natural person designated as its representative by its attorney, or (3) a person whose presence is shown by a party to be essential to the presentation of the party's cause, or (4) a person authorized by statute to be present.

Cases and Authorities

A Rule 615 order usually results from a motion by a party to exclude witnesses. Either of the parties may move the court to exclude witnesses from the courtroom until they are called to the witness stand. Counsel may also request that the witnesses be ordered to not discuss the case with one another, particularly where one witness has testified and the other is waiting to testify.

Once a sequestration order has been issued and a possible violation is claimed, the trial judge must decide whether a violation occurred and the appropriate punishment. C. Gibbons, A Student's Guide to Trial Objections 277 (2003).

If it is determined that a violation has occurred, the court has a range of possible sanctions to choose from. Allowing the offending witness to be vigorously cross-examined about his transgression and instructing the jury in a way that undermines the credibility of the witness are two of these. *United States v. Solorio*, 337 F.3d 580, 592–93 (6th Cir. 2003)(holding that district court's remedies for alleged violation by government witness was appropriately fashioned and within court's discretion where court foreclosed government from eliciting witness's testimony regarding certain information, allowed defendants to explore violation in cross-examination, and instructed jury that it could consider violation in making credibility determinations).

A party who is injured by testimony from a witness who was supposed to be excluded under a Rule 615 order often asks that the offending witness' testimony be stricken. Courts, however, are loath to impose this extreme sanction. See *United States v. Rhynes*, 218 F.3d 310, 321–22 (4th Cir. 2000)(collecting cases and authorities; sanctions for sequestration violation must be proportional to the severity of the offense).

Rule 615 excepts certain persons from mandatory exclusion, once the motion to exclude is granted. Included in this group are people who are the named parties, or designated representatives of corporations or the government, or persons whose presence is essential to the case. The last category is read by many courts to refer primarily to expert witnesses. In addition, the Victims Rights Clarification Act, 18 U.S.C.A. § 3510 provides that victims may not be excluded from the trial simply because of the fact that they may give evidence at a sentencing hearing.

There is some dispute in the cases over whether Rule 615 extends beyond the courtroom to authorize the court to preclude out-of-court communications between witnesses during trial of the case. *United States v. Solorio*, supra. A number of cases permit courts to expand the scope of their orders to control out-of-court witness conversations. For example of such an order, see *United States v. Ortiz*, 10 F.Supp.2d 1058 (N.D. Iowa 1998) (collecting cases and authorities on persons exempted from the rule of exclusion).

Comment

As stated in R. Carlson, E. Imwinkelried, E. Kionka, and K. Strachan, Evidence: Teaching Materials for an Age of Science and Statutes 61 (2002), if a prospective witness violates a sequestration order, in some jurisdictions the judge may penalize the violation by ruling the person incompetent as a witness. However, even in those jurisdictions, the prospective witness' disqualification is not automatic. *Holder v. United States*, 150 U.S. 91, 14 S.Ct. 10, 37 L.Ed. 1010 (1893); *United States v. Cropp*, 127 F.3d 354 (4th Cir. 1997); *United States v. English*, 92 F.3d 909, 913 (9th Cir. 1996); *United States v. Whiteside*, 404 F.Supp. 261, 266 (D. Del. 1975). Some cases hold that automatic disqualification would be too drastic a sanction. The judge has the discretion to decide whether disqualification is the appropriate remedy. In exercising that discretion, the judge considers such factors as whether the witness' violation was inadvertent (*Barnard v. Henderson*, 514 F.2d 744, 745–46 (5th Cir. 1975)) or willful (*United States v. Torbert*, 496 F.2d 154, 158 (9th Cir. 1974)); and how important the prospective witness' testimony is. *Barnard v. Henderson*, supra. Even if the judge decides against disqualifying the prospective witness, he or she can take some remedial action. For example, in the final charge to the jury, the judge may comment on the witness' violation of the sequestration order and give the jury a cautionary instruction about the witness' testimony. *Hill v. Porter Memorial Hosp.*, 90 F.3d 220 (7th Cir. 1996); *United States v. Eastwood*, 489 F.2d 818, 821 (5th Cir. 1973). The judge also has the options of mistrying the case, or holding the witness in contempt. *United States v. Miller*, 499 F.2d 736, 742 (10th Cir. 1974). Carlson, Imwinkelried, Kionka and Strachan, supra at 62. Further, the court can allow the testimony but permit cross-examination about violation of the court order and the effect of any coaching. *United States v. Posada–Rios*, 158 F.3d 832, 871–72 (5th Cir. 1998).

State of Mind

Elements

To prove another individual's state of mind, call a witness who heard the person make declarations about or reflecting upon his mental state. Establish one of these elements: 1) a person's declared state of mind reflects a mental or emotional condition which is relevant to the case; or 2) the person declares an intent to take future action which is relevant to the case, which statement bears on his conduct at a material time.

Cross-Examination

On direct examination in a civil case, a police officer testified on behalf of an injured plaintiff in an auto collision dispute. The officer testified that the defendant fled from the accident scene. The officer is now cross-examined.

Q. (by defense attorney) Officer, you have previously given testimony in this case to the effect that my client purportedly fled the scene of this accident?

A. Yes.

Q. My client didn't just hurry away, though; he said something as he was leaving, didn't he?

A. Yes, that's true.

Q. What, if anything, did the defendant Ed Clifton say immediately as he walked away from the area of the accident?

A. He was addressing me. I heard him say, "I'm concerned about my wife. She will be worried sick if she hears about this. I'm going to find a pay phone and call her right away."

Rule Reference

Federal Evidence Rule 803. Hearsay Exceptions; Availability of Declarant Immaterial. The following are not excluded by the hearsay rule, even though the declarant is available as a witness:

. . .

(3). Then existing mental, emotional, or physical condition

A statement of the declarant's then existing state of mind, emotion, sensation, or physical condition (such as intent, plan, motive, design, mental feeling, pain and bodily health), but not including a statement of memory or belief to prove the fact remembered or believed unless it relates to the execution, revocation, identification, or terms of declarant's will.

Cases and Authorities

United States v. Newell, 315 F.3d 510, 523 (5th Cir. 2002) (holding notes written by defendant's accountant expressing concern over billing practices admissible as evidence of accountant's state of mind at time she confronted defendant where accountant "testified that she authored [notes] when the events were still 'fresh in her mind' "); *E.E.O.C. v. University of Chicago Hospitals*, 276 F.3d 326, 333 (7th Cir. 2002)(testimony that fellow employee told witness "it looked like she was going to get fired" admissible to show the employee's then existing state of mind); *United States v. Reyes*, 239 F.3d 722 (5th Cir. 2001)(not state of mind); *United States v. Serafini*, 233 F.3d 758, 769–70 (3d Cir. 2000)(declarations to witnesses regarding what checks were intended for); *Story v. Sunshine Foliage World, Inc.*, 120 F.Supp.2d 1027, 1032–34 (M.D. Fla. 2000)(nonverbal conduct as reflecting state of mind).

Comment

When the actor in the foregoing trial scenario declared his intent to leave the scene, the declaration is relevant to the issue of whether he fled to evade punishment or rather left for a legitimate purpose. On the hearsay aspect, a longtime exception to the hearsay rule allows a declarant's professed intention to constitute a provable fact in evidence where the planned conduct is relevant. *Mutual Life Insurance Co. v. Hillmon*, 145 U.S. 285, 12 S.Ct. 909, 36 L.Ed. 706 (1892).

Summaries

Elements

In order to introduce a summary of regularly kept data which is voluminous, establish these elements: 1) the case involves voluminous records which, while admissible, cannot conveniently be examined in court; 2) a chart or other form of summary correctly reflects data contained in the underlying records; 3) the underlying records are made available for inspection by the opposing party, and often this is done prior to trial.

Direct Examination

Q. Doctor, how many times has the plaintiff visited your office for medical treatment?

A. 16 times.

Q. Are the records generated by these visits extensive?

A. Yes, many of them are. With the data recorded during each visit, test results, X-ray reports and my own reports, it is quite a stack.

Plaintiff's Attorney: Your honor, since these documents are lengthy, I have made a chart summarizing the data contained in the doctor's reports as well as the office records recording data from each of the 16 visits. This chart will save the jury from going through a lot of records. I will ask a few more questions relevant to the chart. Doctor, I hand you a chart which has been marked plaintiff's exhibit A. Have you compared your data contained in the office records and test results with the depiction on this chart?

A. Yes, I did so at your request.

Q. What did you find?

A. The figures and notations on the chart exactly summarize the essential data in my records.

Plaintiff's Attorney: We offer plaintiff's exhibit A into evidence.

Court: Received.

Rule Reference

Federal Evidence Rule 1006. Summaries.

The contents of voluminous writings, recordings, or photographs which cannot conveniently be examined in court may be presented in the form of a chart, summary, or calculation. The originals, or duplicates, shall be made available for examination or copying, or both, by other parties at reasonable time and place. The court may order that they be produced in court.

Cases and Authorities

A chart which summarizes extensive records is an excellent way to present the data contained in the records. Several points which are significant when introducing summary proof were made in *United States v. Wainright*, 351 F.3d 816, 820–21 (8th Cir. 2003) (finding no abuse of discretion in admission of summary where government witness testified how summary was developed from voluminous records previously introduced into evidence, summary was fair, accurate, correct and non-misleading, defense counsel was allowed to cross-examine witness about the summary, and court gave jury a limiting instruction on use of summary). Another decision approving this form of proof is *United States v. Caballero*, 277 F.3d 1235, 1247 (10th Cir. 2002)(summarized business records and condensed client lists).

Business records are often summarized under this rule. As noted in the Elements section of this entry, there is a requirement that the evidence upon which the summary is based must be admissible.

Some courts will treat summary charts as demonstrative aids only; others will accord them evidentiary status. Holding that charts may go back to the jury room during deliberations, in the discretion of the court, see *United States v. Stephens*, 779 F.2d 232, 238–40 (5th Cir. 1985): "As each chart was introduced, the court instructed the jury that the summary charts did not in themselves constitute evidence in the case; the real evidence was the underlying documents. The judge repeated this instruction in his general charge to the jury, and then the court allowed the summary charts to go into the jury room. . . . In sum, we find that the judge properly admitted the summary charts into evidence under Rule 1006, and consequently there was no error in allowing the charts to go into the jury room with the jury." Accord, *United States v. Johnson*, 54 F.3d 1150 (4th Cir. 1995)(collecting cases and authorities). Contra, *United States v. Meshack*, 225 F.3d 556, 582 (5th Cir. 2000).

Comment

The importance of the court instructing on the limited purpose of the chart was emphasized in *Gomez v. Great Lakes Steel Div., Nat. Steel Corp.*, 803 F.2d 250, 257–58 (6th Cir. 1986). Where the underlying documents are not admissible, or where they are not made available to opposing counsel, courts have been willing to reject summaries. *Air Safety, Inc. v. Roman Catholic Archbishop of Boston*, 94 F.3d 1, 8 (1st Cir. 1996)(party should give notice of its intent to invoke Rule 1006); *Crowder v. Aurora Cooperative Elevator Co.*, 223 Neb. 704, 721, 393 N.W.2d 250, 261 (1986); *Hackett v. Housing Authority of San Antonio*, 750 F.2d 1308, 1312 (5th Cir. 1985).

Related matters, see *Business Records* as well as *Computer Records* in this text. Annotations, see 59 ALR 4th 971; 80 ALR

3d 405, 50 ALR Fed 319. Proof of Facts reference, see 44 Am.
Jur. Proof of Facts 2d 707.

Texts and Treatises

Elements

To cross-examine an expert from a book or text, establish these elements: 1) the book used to examine the witness is a standard in the expert's professional field, or at least it is a recognized authority; 2) the passage from the treatise which is relied upon by the cross-examiner directly contradicts the trial expert's opinions or findings; 3) the cross-examiner confronts the witness with the writing and the witness is afforded an opportunity to deny or explain the inconsistency between her opinions and those of the treatise author.

Cross-Examination

Q. (by defense attorney) You stated on direct examination that you were medically certain that the plaintiff's whiplash would disable him for several years in the future, didn't you?

A. Yes.

Q. In treating the patient, did you make any special studies in the field of cervical sprain injuries?

A. No.

Q. What about studies of nerve root compression in the cervical spine?

A. No.

Q. But you are familiar with Dr. Fielding Hardy's standard text, "Cervical Pain and Sprain?"

A. Yes.

Q. It is well accepted, isn't it?

A. It is a recognized text, yes, but I don't necessarily agree with everything that Hardy says.

Q. How do you square this text statement with your estimation that the injury will persist for years in the future—page 367 of Hardy states: "The prognosis for cervical strain injuries is good where no fracture is present, and most are resolved in a matter of months with conservative therapy which includes heat, muscle relaxants, and support such as a Thomas Collar?"

Rule Reference

Federal Evidence Rule 803. Hearsay Exceptions; Availability of Declarant Immaterial. The following are not excluded by the hearsay rule, even though the declarant is available as a witness:

. . .

(18) Learned treatises. To the extent called to the attention of an expert witness upon cross-examination or relied upon by the expert witness in direct examination, statements contained in published treatises, periodicals, or pamphlets on a subject of history, medicine, or other science or art, established as a reliable authority by the testimony or admission of the witness or by other expert testimony or by judicial notice. If admitted, the statements may be read into evidence but may not be received as exhibits.

Cases and Authorities

For cases on the topic of contradicting an expert with a recognized text, see *Carroll v. Morgan*, 17 F.3d 787, 790 (5th Cir. 1994), which held the cross-examination of a cardiologist was appropriate even though the expert refused to recognize the cross-examiner's treatise as authoritative, where another expert testified it was a reliable authority. Where neither the witness on the stand nor any other expert recognizes the text as a trustworthy treatise, cross-examination from it is disallowed. *Schneider v. Revici*, 817 F.2d 987, 991 (2d Cir. 1987)(holding exclusion of learned treatise correct where defense counsel failed to lay foundation for introduction of text, and noting trial judge's instructions to defense counsel to "[g]et some expert to come in here and testify that it is a recognized treatise as the rule requires" and that "the proper question to the witness is whether that book is recognized in the medical profession as an authoritative book on the treatment of cancer.").

When the expert has referred to some medical authority to sustain her, passages from the authority may be quoted during cross-examination to contradict the witness. Where the doctor has not relied on the published work during his direct examination, counsel may make independent proof of authoritativeness (including asking the witness himself if the work is a recognized one), or may request judicial notice of the book. Related subject, see *Judicial Notice* in this text.

Comment

Proofs for contradiction of expert witnesses through the use of authoritative treatises appear in R. Carlson, Successful Techniques for Civil Trials 2d § 4:45 (1992). Establishing the recognized character of the authoritative treatise to impeach, see 31 Am. Jur. Proof of Facts 2d 443 §§ 7–8. On the other hand, how can the contradiction be met by the proponent of the witness? Advice for countering impeachment when the witness is attacked by psychiatric or medical articles or books is contained in Carlson, supra at § 4:46.

In addition to impeachment, the federal rules allow a recognized treatise to be used by a witness on direct, as an exception to the hearsay rule. Some states, in enacting the federal rules as their own, have adopted the cross-examination pattern but have refused to embrace the Direct Examination formula. Others have followed the federal approach and allow recognized texts on both direct and cross. If admitted, statements from texts may be read into evidence but the text may not be received as an exhibit. Supporting an expert on direct by quotations from a recognized treatise, see *Caruolo v. John Crane, Inc.*, 226 F.3d 46, 55 (2d Cir. 2000)(excerpts of study properly read to jury under learned treatise exception to hearsay rule; fact that this was done on redirect as opposed to direct examination "is of no consequence"); *Tart v. McGann*, 697 F.2d 75, 78 (2d Cir. 1982)(observing that trial judge misapplied rule when judge prohibited use of learned text as substantive evidence and announced it could only be used as a cross-examination tool).

Uncharged Misconduct

Elements

When a prosecutor seeks to place in the record certain instances of prior misconduct by the accused, this "other crimes" proof is often admissible. Foundation facts must establish: 1) the "other crimes" evidence is offered on an issue other than the character of the defendant; 2) a proper witness or documents must be produced to prove the defendant was involved in the other incident; 3) the "other acts" evidence establishes motive for the acts done by the defendant in the present case, or demonstrates an act or acts accomplished in preparation for the charged offense, or helps to establish the defendant acted intentionally and not inadvertently, or is offered for one of the other legitimate purposes for prior misconduct evidence set forth in Rule 404(b).

Direct Examination

Q. (by prosecutor) Mr. Wilcox, about 1 p.m. on July 25, which is about an hour before the food store robbery, did you see anything unusual?

A. Yes. I was looking out the front window of my house and I saw that man (indicating defendant) steal my car.

Q. How can you identify him as the man who stole your car?

Objection by Defense: Irrelevant as well as prejudicial, your honor.

Prosecutor: Preparatory act, your honor. This is prior misconduct which was in preparation for the robbery offense charged in this case.

Court: Overruled.

A. I could tell it was him because of the prominent nose, acne on the face, and the striking red hair. Also, the build and height are the same.

Rule Reference

Federal Evidence Rule 404(b). Other crimes, wrongs, or acts. Evidence of other crimes, wrongs, or acts is not admissible to prove the character of a person in order to show action in conformity therewith. It may, however, be admissible for other purposes, such as proof of motive, opportunity, intent, preparation, plan, knowledge, identity, or absence of mistake or accident, provided that upon request by the accused, the prosecution in a criminal case shall provide reasonable notice in advance of trial, or during trial if the court excuses pretrial notice on good cause shown, of the general nature of any such evidence it intends to introduce at trial.

Cases and Authorities

Normally, criminal procedure rules exclude specific acts of misconduct committed in the past by an accused. Unless they are convictions used to impeach a defendant who testifies, they are inadmissible. These individual acts are not permitted to be proved up in order to establish a defendant's bad reputation, for example. However, Rule 404(b) allows prior acts evidence in limited, specific circumstances. Exceptions to the rule of exclusion include the topics on the following list.

- Motive, see *United States v. Morris*, 287 F.3d 985, 989–990 (10th Cir. 2002)(evidence of other crimes admissible to prove motive and intent). An instruction may be given directing the jury to consider "other crimes" evidence only for a limited purpose. *United States v. Cruz*, 326 F.3d 392, 396 (3d Cir. 2003).

- Opportunity, see *Blind–Doan v. Sanders*, 291 F.3d 1079 (9th Cir. 2002).

- Intent, see *United States v. Morris*, 287 F.3d 985, 989–990 (10th Cir. 2002)(evidence of other crimes admissible to prove motive and intent). A limiting instruction may be given. See *United States v. Cassell*, 292 F.3d 788, 796 (D.C. Cir. 2002).

- Preparation, see *United States v. Arney*, 248 F.3d 984, 992 (10th Cir. 2001)(in bank fraud prosecution where bank loans were secured by cattle, no error in admitting into evidence false cattle inventory reports). In *United States v. Lambert*, 995 F.2d 1006, 1008 (10th Cir. 1993), there was testimony about preliminary conversations between the defendant and another man in which they identified good targets for robberies. When they ultimately robbed a bank, the prior discussions were introduced on the theory that the conversations were necessary preliminary planning for the bank robbery. The court held that "other act" evidence is admissible when inextricably intertwined with the crime on trial, *or when the other acts were necessary preliminaries to the crime charged.*

- Plan, see *United States v. Thompson*, 286 F.3d 950, 968–69 (7th Cir. 2002)(several violent acts alleged to have been perpetrated on or committed by drug conspiracy members admissible to clarify timing of events and to show how drug conspiracy operated).

- Knowledge, see *United States v. Gonzalez*, 328 F.3d 755, 759–60 (5th Cir. 2003)(12–year-old conviction for transporting drugs was employed to demonstrate defendant's knowledge of drugs, and his ability to spot and identify a substance as an illegal drug in the current case); *United States v. Hardy*, 289 F.3d 608, 613 (9th Cir. 2002)(unrelated illicit real estate scheme admissible to show defendant knew goods in question in this case were stolen).

- Identity, see *United States v. Mack*, 258 F.3d 548, 552–54 (6th Cir. 2001)("signature" crimes committed by accused in the past were admissible to show defendant's identity as the perpetrator of the crime charged in this case).

- Absence of mistake or accident, see *United States v. Best*, 250 F.3d 1084, 1092 (7th Cir. 2001)(testimony regarding defendant's prior drug-related activity tended to establish that defendant's presence at the crack house in this case was not the result of a mistake).

Comment

The impetus for prosecutors to offer "other acts" evidence received a boost when the United States Supreme Court ruled that facts underlying prior acquittals of an accused person were not barred when used against him in a later trial. In *Dowling v. United States*, 493 U.S. 342, 110 S.Ct. 668, 107 L.Ed.2d 708 (1990), the Supreme Court held that proof of prior misconduct was admissible notwithstanding the fact that the defendant had been found not guilty. Evidence "relating to an alleged crime that the defendant had previously been acquitted of committing" was admissible in a later proceeding under Rule 404(b) of the Federal Rules of Evidence. After the evidence was admitted, the district judge instructed the jury of the acquittal and advised them the evidence could only be considered for a "limited purpose." When the case reached the Supreme Court, the Court rejected the defendant's contention that it was "fundamentally unfair" to admit this evidence. The defense had urged that the introduction of such "other crimes" testimony "contravenes a tradition that the government may not force a person acquitted in one trial to defend against the same accusation in [another trial]." The Supreme Court disagreed.

An important issue relates to the burden of proof on a prosecutor once the prosecutor notifies the defense of the prosecution's intent to introduce "other crimes" evidence (there is such a notice provision in Rule 404(b)). How much does the trial judge have to be persuaded that the defendant was involved in the other act, in order to allow the jury to hear testimony about the uncharged misconduct? By what measure of proof must the jury be persuaded the defendant did the other crime or wrong, in order to consider the other crime or wrong in the current case? According to *Huddleston v. United States*, 485 U.S. 681, 108 S.Ct. 1496, 99 L.Ed.2d 771 (1988), the judge must preliminarily receive evidence which she deems sufficient for a jury to conclude by a preponderance of the evidence that the defendant committed the other crime, wrong or bad act.

The defendant may object to "other crimes" evidence on relevance grounds as well as objecting to its prejudicial impact. The latter objection will cause the judge to weigh the probative value of the evidence against its emotional effect, under Rule 403. If other acts are admitted, the defendant should request an instruction which limits the purpose for which the evidence may be used. *United States v. Butch*, 256 F.3d 171, 175 (3d Cir. 2001).

What about the age of the prior incident? Is there a bright-line rule of remoteness, a time period beyond which the act of misconduct is deemed too stale to be introduced? The answer to this question is no. There is no *per se* rule which mandates when prior bad acts are too old to be admissible.

Civil Case Applications

While a majority of the decisions under Rule 404(b) are criminal cases, the rule applies in civil actions as well. Further, there is no requirement that the prior bad act be a crime. Accordingly, in a business dispute one of the parties might introduce an episode of bad business practice committed by the opposing party, as long as the incident has independent logical relevance. It does when it illuminates one of the subjects mentioned in Rule 404(b)(motive, opportunity, intent, preparation, plan, knowledge, identity, or absence of mistake).

Judges in cases involving contractual fraud or employment discrimination have invoked Rule 404(b) to admit prior misconduct evidence. In *Hitt v. Connell*, 301 F.3d 240, 249–50 (5th Cir. 2002), evidence of the defendant employer's past discrimination toward union employees was admissible to prove the employer's illegal motive in firing the plaintiff based upon plaintiff's union activity. Past discriminatory discharges of employees were deemed to be probative of the employer's discriminatory intent in a subsequent discharge of the plaintiff in *Epstein v. Kalvin–Miller Int'l, Inc.*, 121 F.Supp.2d 742, 748–49 (S.D.N.Y. 2000). Civil practitioners have come to realize that uncharged misconduct evidence can be highly useful in helping to prove discriminatory intent. *Robinson v. Runyon*, 149 F.3d 507, 513 (6th Cir. 1998).

Other civil cases have found independent logical relevance in prior bad acts. In *Brunet v. United Gas Pipeline Co.*, 15 F.3d 500 (5th Cir. 1994), evidence of prior convictions were admissible to demonstrate that a towboat company was negligent in hiring its crew.

Voice

Elements

Elements of voice identification include: 1) the witness receiving a telephone call recognized the caller's voice at the time, and recalls it now; or 2) the witness received a telephone call and since the time thereof has acquired familiarity with the calling party's voice; 3) the subject of the call is relevant to the case and the conversation escapes the hearsay bar because of an exception or otherwise.

Direct Examination

Q. Who called you on July 23, 2004, if you know?

A. Sloan Smith, the defendant.

Q. How do you know it was Sloan Smith?

A. I know his voice. I had spoken to him at least a dozen times previously, both in person as well as on the telephone.

Rule References

Rule 901(b) of the Federal Rules of Evidence sets forth a nonexhaustive set of examples of the ways in which commonly encountered evidence may be authenticated.

Federal Evidence Rule 901(b)(5) provides as follows: *(5) Voice identification*. Identification of a voice, whether heard firsthand or through mechanical or electronic transmission or recording, by opinion based upon hearing the voice at any time under circumstances connecting it with the alleged speaker.

Federal Evidence Rule 901(b)(6) provides that telephone conversations may be proved by evidence that a call was made to the number assigned at the time by the telephone company to a particular person or business, if (A) in the case of a person, circumstances, including self-identification, show the person answering to be the one called, or (B) in the case of a business, the call was made to a place of business and the conversation related to business reasonably transacted over the telephone.

Cases and Authorities

The usual method of voice identification is to have a witness who heard the party speak tell the trier of fact that he recognizes or recognized the speaker's voice. *United States v. Lampton,* 158 F.3d 251, 257 (5th Cir. 1998). See *United States v. Mansoori,* 304 F.3d 635, 665 (7th Cir. 2002)(holding FBI language specialist's identification of defendants as participants in intercepted and recorded telephone calls admissible even though specialist only heard defendants speak in person once at court proceeding prior to trial, noting that although basis for identification was arguably weak, accuracy is question for jury).

When introducing a sound recording of a telephone conversation or otherwise, a foundation witness will need to identify the voices. If the recording is unduly garbled, it will be rejected. *McAlinney v. Marion Merrell Dow, Inc.,* 992 F.2d 839, 842 (8th Cir. 1993). However, where some of the words are hard to understand courts have broad discretion to permit use of written transcripts to aid jurors in listening to taped conversations. See *United States v. Frazier,* 280 F.3d 835, 849–50 (8th Cir. 2002)(district court did not abuse its power by permitting jury to view transcripts of tape-recorded conversations identifying speakers by name where proponent supplied sufficient voice identification foundation).

Comment

In connection with the telephone, an issue somewhat analogous to whether a letter was sent or received is the question of whether a telephone call was (1) made by a party, or (2) was received by a given person. In the latter case, where the proponent of the telephone call seeks to prove that a certain party received the call, the following rule applies: When the testifying witness dials a phone number listed to X and the person called identifies himself as X, the person answering the phone is presumed to be X if the number was obtained from a telephone book, other reliable information, or from the person allegedly receiving the call.

The foregoing Q. and A. trial proof involves the reverse of this situation. The proponent of the witness seeks to prove identity of the caller. The presumption described in the preceding paragraph is not raised if the witness is a party receiving a call; here the trial question frequently to the recipient of the call is: "What person made the call?" In such cases, if the party receiving the call recognizes the voice of the caller, evidence of the conversation may be admitted if otherwise relevant and admissible under the hearsay rule. Identification of the caller may also be made by circumstantial evidence. See R. Carlson, E. Imwinkelried, E. Kionka & K. Strachan, Evidence; Teaching Materials for an Age of Science and Statutes 236 (5th ed. 2002).

Voice identification also can pose a challenge when a tape recording of a conversation is offered into evidence. Where an appropriate foundation for voice identification is made, tape or wire recordings may be admitted and played to the jury. Editing of sound recordings may affect their admissibility.

The elements that must be satisfied to admit a tape recording into evidence are: (1) a showing that recorder was capable of taking testimony, (2) a showing of the competence of the operator, (3) establishment of the authenticity and correctness of the recording, (4) proof that changes, additions and deletions were not made, (5) proof of the manner of preservation of the recording, (6) proof of identity of the speakers, and (7) a showing that the testimony elicited was voluntary and without inducement. *Furlev Sales & Associates, Inc. v. North American Automotive Warehouse, Inc.*, 325 N.W.2d 20 (Minn. 1982). See *McAlinney*, supra.

Permissibility and standards for use of audio recording to take deposition in state civil case, see 13 ALR 4th 775. Objections to sound recording in criminal cases, see *People v. Sacchitella*, 31 A.D.2d 180, 295 N.Y.S.2d 880 (1968)(tape recording rejected).

In criminal cases, the authorities may have a tape recording which incriminates the accused. In this situation, there is often a need to identify the voices on the tape. Sometimes suspects are brought in and required to speak for identification purposes. This may occur at a lineup or showup. Under most interpretations, this is not a violation of the self-incrimination privilege contained in Amendment V, U.S. Constitution.

What are the distinctions between this topic, voice, and handwriting proof? In Rule 901(b)(2) a rule appears on nonexpert opinion as to handwriting. It carefully stipulates that lay opinion as to the genuineness of handwriting must be based upon familiarity not acquired for purposes of the litigation. Distinction from voice identification is made clear, with the rules on speaker identification allowing the witness to acquire knowledge "at any time under circumstances connecting it with the alleged speaker." The Federal Advisory Committee's Note suggests a reason for the expanded approach to voice identification: "Since aural voice identification is not a subject of expert testimony [under Rule 901(b)(5)], the requisite familiarity may be acquired either before or after the particular speaking which is the subject of the identification, in this respect resembling visual identification of a person rather than identification of handwriting."

For discussion of expert identification of voices, see *State v. Williams*, 4 Ohio St.3d 53, 446 N.E.2d 444, 4 Cal. W. Int'l L.J. 144, 4 Ohio B, 144 (1983)(voice analysis and identification testimony; admissibility of expert testimony such as spectrographic voice analysis). For other identifications of voices, see *Vouras v. State*, 452 A.2d 1165, 1168 (Del. 1982), where an experienced police officer had several opportunities to hear the defendant speak. Further, the officer relied not only upon the defendant's nickname in making the identification but also upon characteristics, mannerisms, and phrases he had heard the defendant use before.

Proof of Facts reference, see 23 Am. Jur. Proof of Facts 3d 315.

Wills [Statements Regarding]

Elements

To contest or support a will when claims like undue influence or lack of testamentary capacity are issues, the testator's declarations are important. They can be proved by establishing: 1) the testator spoke in the presence of or within the hearing of the trial witness; 2) the testator's declarations are relevant to the issues involved in the will case; 3) the trial witness can recall and relate the testator's words, and can identify the time and place where they were uttered.

Direct Examination

Q. What, if anything, did the testator say about the making of his will?

A. He said he was still under a lot of mental stress and that his nephew had threatened to use force unless he signed the will.

Q. The record in this case shows the will was signed on July 1, 2004. When did the conversation which you referred to occur?

A. It was around August 18, 2004, his 70th birthday. I was at his house to wish him "Happy Birthday" and give him a present.

Rule Reference

Federal Evidence Rule 803. Hearsay Exceptions; Availability of Declarant Immaterial. The following are not excluded by the hearsay rule, even though the declarant is available as a witness:

. . .

(3) Then existing mental, emotional, or physical condition. A statement of the declarant's then existing state of mind, emotion, sensation, or physical condition (such as intent, plan, motive, design, mental feeling, pain and bodily health), but not including a statement of memory or belief to prove the fact remembered or believed *unless it relates to the execution, revocation, identification, or terms of declarant's will* [emphasis added].

Cases and Authorities

See *State v. Gabusi*, 149 N.H. 327, 821 A.2d 1064, 1066–69 (2003)(holding testimony by decedent's doctor, attorney, and social worker regarding decedent's repeated statements that he intended to take care of his sister were relevant to demonstrate decedent's belief that his wishes would be carried out after he died, and admissible under the hearsay exception to show that subsequent execution of a will without such provision as well as execution of power of attorney to the defendant probably resulted from deception). It is important in a will contest case to present witnesses who can report the testator's declarations which were made to them both before and after a will's execution. The testator's intentions and state of mind are reflected in these declarations. Accordingly, a large number of American jurisdictions admit a testator's declarations which were made around the time he executed his will. As stated in R. Carlson, E. Imwinkelried, E. Kionka & K. Strachan, Evidence: Teaching Materials for an Age of Science and Statutes 510 (2002), "there is a special need for the testator's declarations. *Lewis v. Lewis*, 241 Miss. 83, 129 So.2d 353 (1961). It is normally difficult to prove a person's state of mind; and the proponent usually resorts to this hearsay exception when the declarant, the testator or testatrix, is already deceased. The declarant's death creates an especially compelling justification for resorting to hearsay evidence. There may be doubts about the declarant's memory and sincerity, but most jurisdictions have concluded that the need for the evidence outweighs the doubts. That conclusion explains the concluding clause in Federal Rule 803(3)."

Comment

While the hearsay rule in the general run of cases often precludes a declarant's statements which face backward and not forward, an exception is made for will cases. Most jurisdictions allow statements of present memory to prove past events in estate litigation. Federal Evidence Rule 803(3) provides that the hearsay rule does not preclude a witness from testifying to a declarant's statements which related to the execution of the declarant's will. There is a special need to receive a testator's declarations. Thus, the testator's statement in the foregoing Q. and A. about mental stress as well as his nephew are admissible.

In estate litigation, the related topics of lay opinion as to testamentary capacity as well as experts in will cases are located in R. Carlson, Successful Techniques for Civil Trials 2d §§ 4:17, 4:39 (1992). Proof of Facts reference, testamentary capacity, see 40 Am. Jur. Proof of Facts 2d 339. Proving undue influence, see 36 Am. Jur. Proof of Facts 2d 109.

X-rays

Elements

To introduce and use an X-ray, establish these elements: 1) that the physician or a qualified technician took the X-rays; 2) the witness, an expert, can identify the X-ray as one taken of the person involved in the litigation; 3) the interpretation of the X-ray is accomplished by a competent and qualified professional.

Direct Examination

Q. (by the plaintiff's attorney near end of qualifications of doctor). Has your medical practice required you to interpret X-rays?

A. Yes.

Q. Will you please describe that?

A. I have been in private practice as an orthopedist for about 2 years, and during that time I have seen over 200 patients; in virtually every case I consulted and interpreted X-rays.

Counsel: Your honor, I request permission to approach the witness.

Court: Granted.

Q. I now hand you what has been marked plaintiff's exhibit 1 for identification. What is it?

A. An X-ray picture of the left hip joint of the plaintiff, Helene X. Crass.

Q. Dr. Wingfield, have you seen this X-ray before?

A. Yes.

Q. Where?

A. At St. Francis Emergency Hospital.

Q. Under what circumstances?

A. I studied this film on July 2, 2004, a few minutes after it was taken. Ms. Crass had come into the emergency room, and I reviewed the film in order to treat Ms. Crass. I undertook her care, and I deemed the X-ray procedure to be necessary to accurately diagnose her case. She reported that she had fallen, and was in severe pain radiating from her left hip.

Q. How do you know that this X-ray is of the plaintiff?

A. I was there when the technician took the X-rays of Ms. Crass. When the film was developed, I saw him affix the identifying notation on the right lower portion (indicating), which he routinely does.

Counsel: We offer plaintiff's exhibit 1 for identification into evidence as plaintiff's exhibit 1.

Court: It will be admitted.

Q. Doctor, directing your attention to plaintiff's exhibit 1, does it reveal any fractures?

A. (at this point a light box is set up facing the jury; the doctor leaves the witness chair and stands with a pointer) The left femur, or thigh bone, has been broken at the neck. The dark portion shows a substantial fracture line. We see this indicated by the broad dark line running through the neck of the femur **(indicating)**. At this time there has been significant displacement of the proximal or upper part of the femur, evidenced by the portion jutting over here **(again showing with pointer)**. Normally, we would see the top of the femur pictured about here **(indicating)**.

(doctor proceeds to detail the severity of the injury)

Rule Reference

Federal Evidence Rule 901. Requirement of Authentication or Identification.

(a) General provision. The requirement of authentication or identification as a condition precedent to admissibility is satisfied by evidence sufficient to support a finding that the matter in question is what its proponent claims.

Cases and Authorities

See 38 Am. Jur. Proof of Facts 2d 145. A foundation for X-rays may be provided by the patient's attending physician, or by a radiologist or X-ray technician who took the X-ray. With a proper foundation, X-rays are admissible. *Redd v. State*, 240 Ga. 753, 757, 243 S.E.2d 16, 19 (1978).

Normally an expert is the one who lays the foundation for an X-ray. However, occasionally courts are less strict regarding the authenticating witness. See *Jones v. State*, 111 S.W.3d 600, 607 (Tex. App. 2003)(holding accident victim could introduce her own X-rays taken before and after surgeries where victim had personal knowledge about injuries and treatment and where plate and screws used to treat broken leg and shattered ankle were clearly evident, but noting that lay witnesses, even if X-rays are their own, do not have requisite personal knowledge to interpret them).

Comment

Interpretation of films is regularly done by a physician. The authenticating proof may be completed by an X-ray technician. Alternatively, identifying and introducing X-rays may be provided by the party's own treating physician. This is the case where the physician was present when the X-rays were taken. Case support for counsel's introduction of X-rays can be found in the Annotation at 5 ALR 3d 303.

Stipulating the admissibility of X-rays is the norm in many locations. As observed in Lay, *The Use of Real Evidence*, 37 Neb. L. Rev. 501, 510 (1958), "[i]t should never be necessary to take the time of the jurors and the court in the trial of a lawsuit to lay the foundation for an X-ray photograph unless there is some unusual circumstances or objection involved."

Interpretation of the films follows the authentication process in the chronology of proof. As in the Q. and A. example displayed in this entry of the text, a physician will be a frequent witness supplying interpretation, and the trier of fact will be instructed by her on what the abnormalities in the X-rays reflect. See R. Carlson, Successful Techniques for Civil Trials § 3:11 (1992).

†